I've Gotta Pack

Fun Travel Tales That Will Get YOU Planning a Trip

Laura R. Holmes

Content Queens, LLC
Spring Lake, MI

© 2011 Laura R. Holmes

Published by
Content Queens, LLC
Spring Lake, Michigan

Publisher's Cataloging-in-Publication Data
Holmes, Laura R.

I've gotta pack : fun travel tales that will get you planning a trip / by Laura R. Holmes. – Spring Lake, MI : Content Queens, LLC, 2011.

p. ; cm.

ISBN13: 978-0-9846481-0-8

1. Holmes, Laura R.—Travel. 2. Travel—Anecdotes. I. Title.

G465 .H65 2011
910.4—dc22   2011936337

FIRST EDITION

Project coordination by Jenkins Group, Inc.
www.BookPublishing.com

Cover & interior design by Yvonne McKessy
Cover photography by Troy Wells, www. riversedgephoto.com

Printed in the United States of America
15 14 13 12 11 • 5 4 3 2 1

"To experience new places
with friends and to meet new people is a joy,
and in those moments the smile on your face,
will be as wide and as genuine
as any smile you will find!"

—Laura R. Holmes

Contents:

Prologue and Author's Note

Prologue

In the process of writing this book, I have been blessed by many dear friends and family who have imparted much wisdom to me over many years. Usually, it revolves around how we all should strive to be unselfish and balance our lives between key elements: family and friends, career, faith, and fun. This book is mostly about the last item—FUN! The other elements are mixed in, but what is life without joy and fun? My wish for you is that you truly have fun reading this book.

Author's Note

At some point while writing and editing my travel stories into the beginnings of a book, it occurred to me that my wanderlust was completely self-serving. I actually began to feel guilty. I can't pinpoint the exact moment, but I am pretty sure it was a late, sleepless night in the winter of 2007 that a notion popped into my head: I needed to make this "book project" less self-serving. "What if I made a pact with myself now to donate 50% of any profits made as a result of any book sales to family or charities?" I continued on this thought process, and my eyes widened in the dark. My mind churned a bit more, and I thought perhaps it would be $100 or maybe $100,000 donated, but I made a deal with myself that night to stick to this plan no matter the level or lack of success. Other details, such as picking charities, I thought I could get to later, but, of course, conservancy came to mind and other organizations dedicated to helping people in crisis across the world. So, armed with the inspiration that my little travel book just might do some good, other than being a hobby for me, I was motivated to continue writing and make this into reality.

This book is dedicated to the dear friends and family whom I shared these experiences with and to people who endeavor to experience the world, its vast scenery, and its people. I have found that traveling requires a sense of humor, an open mind, and lots of patience. No matter whether I am traveling in my own state, in country, or internationally, on each trip I always learn a bit more about myself and how I fit into the world. Getting outside west Michigan has provided some worldly perspective and open-mindedness that I would not have without my travel experiences.

I am truly blessed to have visited places around the world. Africa taught me my limits (physically and mentally), Costa Rica taught me to be patient and flexible, Alaska inspired a sense of awe,

Arizona rekindled memories of past family trips, Vegas made me long for greener pastures, Park City and the Rocky Mountains taught me to adapt to rapidly changing conditions, and the Peruvian jungle and Incan ruins brought ancient history to life for me. At some point, I realized I had to write all these travels down so I would not forget the details. For each destination I've visited, each writing exercise provides valuable insight for me and a way to chronicle many unforgettable memories! I am continuing to write, and in volume II, I plan to detail adventures to Italy, Spain, France, Ireland, and other exciting locations.

This is my account of stories, being out of doors, seeing and doing things firsthand–and something I hope will be enlightening to a seasoned adventurer or an exuberant beginner. My advice to you is to plan a trip and get out there and see for yourself. I have found that travel has the ability to change people in positive ways, and it redefines your perspective on the world and its people. I can only hope you enjoy reading these accounts as much as I enjoyed visiting each unique destination.

I would also like to note that while traveling in Africa or whitewater rafting in Costa Rica or hiking in Alaska, I was not pecking away at the keys of a laptop but rather writing down my experiences and chronicles with a pen into my journal at each day's end. It was only later that my scribbles were entered into the digital world to share. The original journal is quite a sight and, as you can imagine, very valuable to me, though it looks as if I have sent it through the washing machine several times. In fact, while rafting in Costa Rica on the Reventezon River, my journal came close to becoming a casualty: it was in my pack and tucked inside a dry bag for our day's journey through white water. That day, our guided raft that held our baggage capsized, flipped over, and floated down the river a half mile before our group was able to turn it over in a shallow area. Only later in the day did I open my pack and pull out my journal to find it soaked through, with much of the ink running and blurring on many pages. I carefully let it dry, and, thankfully, with some effort, I was able to decipher what I had written. That journal is now safely tucked away on a bookshelf, since its pages are full. Now, several new editions have taken its place, and their blank pages await my pen.

Laura has been a traveler and fun-seeker from a very young age to now! Her first trip was with her mom and dad to Nogales, Mexico when she was 6 1/2 months old.

CHAPTER 1

My Introduction to Travel

I've often thought it amazing when you meet or hear about someone who has lived in one particular county or town and has never set foot outside that boundary to take a look around. From my perspective, it seems a sin not to get off the couch and see what is out there– and believe me, there is much to see and people who are incredibly interesting all over the world. For me, I eagerly plot and scheme to leave the place that I call home, not because I don't like it here in west Michigan but because I think I have a traveling heart, one that longs to see new places and experience new cultures. After a divorce (in March 1999) and looking for positive diversions with my newfound freedom and flexibility, it seemed a great idea to be a bit more spontaneous with my time.

So, I developed a habit of adventure traveling in 2001 or thereabout, spearheaded by a friend who "talked me into" a trip over much wine one evening (which is in itself an amusing story that I wrote down and will share as well). I was talked into a visit to Africa–not a bad beginning to traveling abroad. I visited Tanzania for two weeks of incredible sights and experiences that I have yet to match on other trips. That trip was my first true global adventure, and since returning home from Africa (two weeks prior to the events of 9/11), my mind is often wondering where my travels will take me next.

I should back up a bit, though, and give a bit of a history lesson on how I learned to travel as a youngster. I know that at a young age, I learned to appreciate the planning and participation of taking a vacation. At the early age of 6 1/2 months (of course with help from my parents, Marshall and Becky Holmes), I crossed the border into Mexico from

Arizona for my first road trip. I was born in southern Arizona at Fort Huachuca's Raymond W. Bliss Army Hospital, where my dad, finishing a stint in the army, was stationed. He and my mom had a weekend holiday, so they loaded me up in the car and crossed the border at Nogales. We spent the day, and my parents bought me a sombrero, which, of course, I put on and promptly posed for a picture. I love this photo because I have a huge silly grin on my face and that expression reminds me how I feel now when traveling to new places. Though I have no memory of this trip other than this photo, it was a starting point for many travels for me. Shortly after my dad was released from duty, we flew to Michigan, back to my parents' home and family. Once back in Michigan, my little brother, Ben, arrived when I was 4 and my sister, Charla, when I was 9, which meant I had play partners for adventures at home or on the road.

My parents' version of vacationing when I was a youngster was one of camping in the good ole US of A's network of campgrounds, armed with a Dodge Reliant K-car and a pop-up camper. Each summer, with the red K-car's bumper dragging to the blacktop, we loaded bikes on top and stuffed suitcases and supplies inside and then piled in the backseat, full of anticipation of sights to see. My dad was at the wheel, and my mom was armed with maps and brochures. They would chart a course for scenic pullouts, picnic lunches roadside, and a timely arrival to a mosquito-infested state forest campground. Most of my memories of family trips are good ones, filled with searching for firewood, building campfires, roasting hotdogs and marshmallows over embers, and sleeping under the stars to sounds of crickets, Lake Michigan waves, and overzealous raccoons.

One memory that always sticks out in my mind as particularly amusing is a camping trip in northern Michigan. We had arrived at a campground fairly late, and in the haste of setting up our pop-up camper, we must have forgotten to secure a few of the straps on one side, where the canvas stretched around the corners of the side bed. In any case, we all used the bathroom, brushed our teeth, said our good nights, and promptly fell asleep. I was sharing space on one side with Ben, and my mom and dad slept on the other side. At some point late in the night, Ben rolled over and had gotten himself next to the edge, and as he turned in his sleep, the unstrapped canvas edges gave way and he fell, sleeping bag and all, about 3 or 4 feet to the ground. My mom, the light sleeper of the bunch, must have heard the thump. She sat up quickly and rushed to see what had happened. The impact must not have caused too much damage or the sleeping bag softened his fall, because by my mom's description, Ben was just fine and slept through his tumble. She got him back into bed, and I think I may have slept through the entire drama. Unlike my mom, Ben was not a light sleeper. That mishap still manages to resurface over stories told at family holidays, and we laugh about his fall to this day.

Outside of a few mishaps, my dad had made a science of setting up camp, picking the best site, leveling the camper, and making friends with campground rangers and neighbors. At each new campsite, my brother and sister and I would scramble out of the car upon arrival and promptly explore our proximity to the toilets, the beach, and the water pump. But, as much fun as camping was, it required a fair amount of work, especially at mealtime and during teardown and set up, which seemed an endless cycle. I will always wonder how we fit all of us in a K-car with luggage, a Coleman stove, fishing poles, bikes, floaties … difficult to fathom. I think my mom's true genius shone through in those times when she managed our crew, consisting of a restless husband and kids who were always ready to get going to the next stop. I became a travel expert, and car games were a necessity, as I logged thousands of miles in that backseat. I completed entire projects on trips, one where Charla and I made a 6-foot chain made completely out of gum wrappers folded origami style and carefully intersected one-by-one to form our craft. I cannot even guess how many packs of gum we chewed to have the material to finish that endeavor. I do remember having contests to see who could blow the largest bubble. We also kept a careful log of license plates from each state, and we keenly watched each car passing by to see whether a new state would be represented. We were well equipped with all sorts of travel games and books, and when those got boring, we would pick on each other until my dad's hand would reach back and start slapping thighs to let us know we had crossed the line.

The starting point for all this fun was Traverse City, Michigan, and our initial trips included nearby Canada and Michigan's Upper Peninsula. We branched out to other states as we got older. When Charla was added into the mix when I was 9, both Ben and I, by then seasoned campers, looked forward to teaching her the ropes. We collected stickers for our camper as we visited each state and landmark, and we blazed a blistering trail of sights seen. We visited landmark tourist traps such as Tequamenon and Niagara Falls and upper Michigan's famous Mystery Spot. I have very vivid memories of walking through this tilted and uneven house, built on an angle; it seemed to boggle our young minds. We were treated by our tour guide to a demonstration of how water rolls uphill, only in that spot. It was crazy, I thought at the time, and certainly mysterious. Another notable–and the family photo album can prove this–is a visit to the Porkies, better known as the Porcupine Mountains, overlooking Lake Superior in the far western side of Michigan's Upper Peninsula. My family also made trips each May to the Boyne area for the National Morel Mushroom Hunting Festival. If you have heard people talking about picking morel mushrooms, you'd know it is a popular cult hobby in Michigan and in the Midwest. Both my parents had grown up picking morels in northern Michigan woods, so this knack and skill had been passed onto me. At the Boyne Festival, each of us in our family entered in our respective age categories and participated in the timed hunt for fabulous cash prizes and invaluable morel sculptures made out of wood. The "hunt" was very official, and believe it or not, a police officer with flashing lights would escort the caravan of pickers out to a preselected spot. Once all of us were out of the vehicles and ready to go, a horn would go off, and we all sprinted into the woods and started collecting the precious fungi. On many occasions, my dad, mom, or any of us kids collected trophies for winning or placing in our division. I actually won first place one year, and my dad had gotten so good at hunting they made him enter the "pro division." I had never imagined that one could go pro at morel picking. We were a bona fide champion morel-hunting family, and my parents still have the wood carvings etched with our names to prove it.

We diversified and also rode the ferries, for which Michigan is famous, with all our great lakes, to Michigan's Beaver and Mackinaw islands for excursions, and we even stuck out the four-hour trip across Lake Michigan on the USS Badger to Wisconsin to visit my Aunt Sharon, Uncle Joe, and cousins. Once in Milwaukee, all my cousins and I got to see our first metropolitan zoo, complete with my first glimpses of tigers, monkeys, snakes, and the like.

In my early teens, the Holmes family vacation covered the entire Midwest and progressed onward to New Hampshire and northern Maine in a sweep of the upper eastern side. It was there that I made my maiden voyage into the waves of the Atlantic Ocean and enjoyed my first lobster dinner. We also fit in a two-week trip to the Badlands and Black Hills and visited Wall Drug and the Corn Palace on the way. The car ride on that trip was murderous, and I thought I might die of boredom while watching row after row of corn go by in Iowa and South Dakota. After two days of excruciatingly long stints in the car, we finally arrived late afternoon at an area overlooking a riverbed near our campground, the scene of an embarrassing moment for me. Once we had stopped, I literally shot out of the car, and I took off on a full sprint and headed for the river that beckoned me down in a shallow valley about a hundred yards ahead. I paid no attention to my mom, who yelled for me to wait, and I sped on toward the river. I was euphoric to be out of the car, and I picked up speed as I ran on through the sun-baked river valley. I had just about reached my destination and thought about slowing down, but my last step landed and made contact with a slick layer of mud underneath the dry outer layer. In one swift motion, my foot shot out from under me, and, paired with my rate of speed, my body followed airborne and I landed cartoonlike flat on my back in a splat of red mud. My entire backside from head to toe was coated in a slimy mixture of slick red mud, and I lay there for a moment in shock of what had just happened. I had begun to pick myself up and was flicking chunks of mud from my fingertips; to make things worse, my family had caught up and had burst into laughter at my muddy spill. I had made it to the river first all right and was also the first of my family to take a bath in it.

Our other trips included the Western mountain tour, which included the Grand Tetons, Yellowstone Park, and the Rockies. On the Yellowstone trip, we stopped in Helena to visit my Aunt Sharon, Uncle Joe, and my cousin Quenby again, who had moved there from Milwaukee and now lived on a horse ranch overlooking the Elk Horn Mountain range. We spent a few days hanging out with Quenby and played with her pet Border collie and billy goat–no joke. We spent our afternoons tubing down a chilly mountain stream through mild white water and splashing through a tunnel to a stop at the bottom of the hill. Another first for me occurred on this trip: I rode my first horse. I slipped my foot in a stirrup and slid in the saddle for a trot and enjoyed a trail ride with our group around the perimeter of the Madsen Ranch.

Next up was a turn south toward the Mammoth Cave, OpryLand, the Appalachian Trail, and, of course, the Blue Ridge Parkway winding through the Blue Ridge Mountains. On some of these trips, I was old enough to appreciate these places and vistas; others were simply a checkmark on a map in my mom's purse. In any case, for any kid between the ages of 5 and 14, I would consider myself a well-seasoned camper under the tutelage of mom and dad.

As I made my way into my rebellious teens, the family vacation was taken to new heights with the addition of a 24-foot used RV that my dad had proudly purchased. We had graduated to RV camping, and my parents promptly started planning the ultimate destination. To my horror, they announced that the family would take a week that summer and visit Charlotte, North Carolina, to stay at the PTL (Praise the Lord) headquarters' Fort Heritage Resort and Water Park. I was shocked. I was about to spend my summer vacation in the vicinity of the crazy Tammy Faye Baker, who cried, prayed, and spewed black mascara all down her face, all on national television. Despite my angry protests and comments saying "Can't we go somewhere cool?" I was unsuccessful in deterring my parents. The RV was stocked and loaded, and I pouted but tried to make the best of it. We arrived in the blistering hot South and drove through the entrance of the PTL and followed manicured roads into the campground area. Camping there was not so rustic but in the midst of a teeming city with smiling parents and energetic kids everywhere. I volunteered to chaperone Ben and Charla at the kids' area and water park most every day and did everything I could to avoid activities that were anywhere near the PTL Worship Center Complex. I was mostly successful, but my mom and grandma, who had joined us on this trip, announced one night at dinner that they had gotten tickets for the whole family to see a live taping of the Jim and Tammy show the next night. So, of course, we all had to wear our Sunday best for this event, and my mom marched us all over to the facility among hundreds of others, all of whom apparently looked excited at the prospect. I was the "doubting Thomas" of the group and had decided that the whole thing was just "too much" and too "over the top" to be real. My theory would prove to be true years later, but at that moment, I sat and watched, live–PTL evangelism and money making in its heyday. As I fidgeted in my seat, I witnessed tearful testimonies and prayer, hand-clapping hymns, impassioned messages, and hands held high in spiritual acknowledgement. And true to form, Tammy, with microphone in hand, blubbered on about forgiveness and love through her tears, all the while patting at her mascara-stained cheeks. I was moved, as were many people in the audience, but I was moved by the absurdity of this spectacle. Luckily, that night was near the end of the week, so, shortly after, we packed up and headed north. I could not wait to return home and get back to work at my summer job and something more normal.

Oh, but there's more. The spring before the summer of my sweet 16, I had to endure another destination that was not to my liking. As a typical rebellious teenager, I had unsuccessfully tried to convince my dad to let me and three friends drive to Florida for spring break. I was given an "absolutely not," especially when our trip plan lacked an adult chaperone. In hindsight, I laugh at the absurdity of my request of even asking permission to go, but I didn't deserve the alternative plan that was handed to me. Plan B turned out to be a trip with my Grandma Warren to Tulsa, Oklahoma, to visit my cousins Chuck and Cheri, who had just had their first baby, Ashley. Don't get me wrong, I love my grandma, but this was spring break! But, before I could protest, plane tickets were booked, and my Grandma Warren and I flew from Grand Rapids to Chicago in a thunderstorm and were subsequently delayed and missed our connection at O'Hare to Tulsa. So, my first O'Hare experience included missing a flight, waiting in line to rebook, and then taking a hair-raising cab ride to a seedy hotel, all the while starving to death, with my grandma in tow. We did manage to order a pizza, so we ate and watched television for a bit. We made it out on a flight the next morning and arrived in sunny Tulsa and were greeted by my cousins. I made the best of my spring break and hung out by the pool, worked on my tan like it was a job, and played a lot with baby Ashley.

I think that about covers it, at least through my teenage years. I credit my parents for getting out to see the states and dragging me and my brother and sister along with them. I guess my own pioneering spirit was born, with an eager heart and anticipation of trips to come in my future that I, myself, would plan.

So, I'll fast forward to 2001 and my friend Theresa and her coercive powers and how one evening filled with many glasses of wine started me toward Africa. I met Theresa through a mutual friend and coworker, Yvonne, who had talked me into playing indoor soccer. I met my new team and teammate Theresa, whom I began to chat with and get to know during many evenings of postgame euphoria at local watering holes where we discussed our athletic prowess on the field. So, on one such night, she described a trip she had been planning, and for some unexplainable reason, she had not talked anyone else into going to date. Hmmmm? I should have made a mental note to myself. She must have surmised by my soccer-playing ability that I had enough athletic ability and endurance to do some mountain hiking, so she sprung it on me. "What do you think about going to Africa and climbing Mount Kilimanjaro with me?" So there it was, and it was out. I was pretty surprised she asked me, even though I was a bit buzzed. It seems funny to me now: she did not know me particularly well, but she plowed forward and proceeded to describe in great detail the trip itinerary. I distinctly remember her taking a notepad and excitedly drawing me a map of Africa, complete with the location of Mount Kilimanjaro, the route from the states, and a cost estimate on the bottom of the page.

I hadn't done any serious mountain climbing at that point, or even walking at elevation, come to think of it, but when I mentioned this, she simply assured me that though its peak at 19,500 feet seemed extreme, it was a very manageable walk to the summit. With this explanation, she made a gesture with her hands where her fingers touched at the top and her hands and wrists formed a slight slope, indicating the angle of the mountain. She assured me that it was not a technical climb and that, with a good training program, we could jog to the top. We would later laugh out loud at our arrogance of conquering Kili. But the result of the evening was twofold: I had cemented a new friendship, and I had in my mind decided that I must go on this trip. In the next few months, I wondered how I would pay for this trip, and after each soccer game, Theresa and I would buy instant lottery tickets in hopes of financing my adventure. After many discussions at lunches, we made arrangements with Mountain Travel Sobek to do a two-week trip in Tanzania, which included a one-week safari in the state's three main national parks and then a Kilimanjaro hike in week 2. I made a down payment, and documents and itineraries promptly arrived with a two-page list of the vaccinations I needed to get so I could visit Africa. Of course, I also had to complete a health questionnaire and even have my general physician sign off that I was not on the verge of a heart attack. I spent the summer getting in as good of shape as a flatlander can be; Theresa and I jogged and climbed dunes and stairs to try to get our legs ready for six to eight hours of hiking per day to come. As with most of my summers, I also fit in a healthy dose of beach volleyball on Grand Haven beaches and many Saturday tournaments, which I hoped would boost my endurance. That paired with running and dune climbing had me feeling pretty fit as August rolled around.

Photos top to bottom: Mountain biking down a big hill in West Virginia near the New River Gorge; Hiking in southern Arizona; White water rafting in Costa Rica on the Pacuare River.

CHAPTER 2

Wild Africa
Tanzania, Africa–August 2001

August 9, 2001: Day 1

I remember thinking, "Holy crap–I am on a plane to Africa!" I had said it many times, but it was still hard to believe that I was finally on the way to wild Africa. On the way out, I had my first experience in dealing with a travel "bitch attack" from my travel mate, Theresa, in Detroit. Travel requires a lot of patience and planning, and sometimes when those wear thin and are paired with hunger, your mood can quickly go south. Theresa must have gotten a little shaky from lack of nourishment after all the waiting in the airport, so we found a bar and ordered her some potato skins and a Corona, and her disposition improved. In the crisis, I managed to snag only one potato skin and then realized I was also starving. But, I had been smiling all day because I was so excited. I was so glad that Theresa talked me into this vacation. As I thought about this trip (even before I knew what was in store), I knew it would hold a very special place in my memory and that it would be a great story once I returned home. That day marked a very long stint on a plane–at least 10 hours to Amsterdam–so I buckled up and tried to be patient. Theresa had taken a sleeping pill, and she lay sleeping happily in her seat while I sat completely awake to the sounds of crying babies and clearing throats, as well as an occasional shove on my seat from my neighbor behind me.

Day 2

The date had changed, but I was still on the damn plane. Since we flew out at night from Detroit and had now flip-flopped day and night, I officially had experienced significant jet lag. "Are we ever going to get off this plane?" I thought as I sat restlessly in my seat. I remember the announcement of only two hours to Kilimanjaro Airport, but everyone aboard was restless. Since the transfer in Amsterdam, I did one crossword puzzle, watched a movie, tried to sleep, and got pushed around by the people behind my seat, so my excitement had waned. I also passed some time sending glaring looks down my row of seats to a bratty young boy who was loud and back-talking to his mother. My disapproving looks finally got his attention, and I held my "death look" stare until he shut up. Massive hunger pains also plagued me in the last hours; the airlines kept us on a strict caloric intake to save a few dollars, and I could not figure out which meal I had missed, lunch or dinner? All would be well when we touched down, so until then I tried to be patient. Next to me, Theresa had Barbara Streisand on her CD player to pass the time, and she kept our area smelling "rosy" with a steady spritz of rose-scented spray here and there. After 10 hours and the stench of hundreds of people on the plane, of which I was no exception, I was ready to land.

Group members included Laura, Theresa, Susie, Michelle, Barbara, Linda, Alice, Denny, and Bob. Our guides were Godfrey, Ellie, and Richard from Mountain Travel Sobek.

We arrived at Kilimanjaro International Airport in Tanzania in the dark, so it was still hard to believe we were there, in Africa, but the hum of new voices and strange new languages cemented the fact. Our trip leaders, Godfrey and Ellie, who were all smiles, introduced themselves and led us to a car, and we drove 30 minutes to the Dik Dik Lodge in Arusha. Even with only headlights illuminating the entrance, the grounds were beautiful, with trimmed hedges and bright flowers lining the way in. We met our group and had dinner, which consisted of beef, soup, and potatoes, which was not at all what I expected. I think I was prepared for some strange game or exotic vegetable that I would be worried to try. I even had a local brew called Kilimanjaro Lager, which was very good. Everyone was travel weary, so the chat wound down and Godfrey gave us our morning meet time. Day 2 came to an end when we were escorted by incredibly polite staff to room 14, a well-appointed room with netting around two very comfortable beds. Theresa and I did "rock-paper-scissors" for the first shower, and we agreed we should take a sleeping pill to be ready and rested for the safari start the next day. Theresa had brought along some prescription sleep aids, so I took her advice and popped one before hopping into bed. I rarely take anything to help me sleep, and now I know why. I woke up several hours later, in a panicked sweat, feeling as if I were hyperventilating, along with a pounding heart. I rushed into the bathroom to splash some water on my face and try to calm down. All the while, Theresa slept peacefully in her bed and never noticed my panic attack. It finally passed after forcing some slower breaths through my lungs. I told Theresa about my mishap the next morning and thanked her sarcastically for talking me into taking a sleeping pill. She laughed at me and surmised that the sleep aid, paired with a beer and my low resting heart rate, had produced overly relaxing effects on my body. My heart rate must have dropped a bit too low during sleep, which may have caused my pounding heart and panic attack. Well, I survived the first night in Africa–but just barely.

Day 3: Savannah Breezes

"Today, I will feel the breeze from the African savannah on my face," I thought as I readied my day pack. At 9 a.m., I ate breakfast with the group and enjoyed Westernized food such as bread, eggs, coffee, and so on. Godfrey led a quick briefing and told us where we would be heading and what to expect. We were told to "ask to check the tire pressure" if we had to pee while on safari (the number 1 safari code). After a few other tips, we loaded up our gear into tow Land Rovers and drove two hours to Tarangire National Park. It was my first experience on African roadways, and the start was fine on blacktop, but we progressed to more and more rutted red dirt roads while going remarkably fast. We arrived around noon, and it quickly got very warm, so sunscreen and safari hats were donned by all. The vehicles had open roofs so you could stand and watch or take pictures with a better vantage point. It was difficult to describe the feeling you have when you see your first African animal. For me, it was the zebra, and not only was it unique to this landscape but also the sheer numbers of them in this park held my gaze for quite some time. The only wildlife I saw at home was an occasional turkey or some deer. Thousands of zebras grazed, some mere yards away and many more in the distance on the flat plains area to our west. For many hours, we followed a two-track road winding its way through the park, all the while in anticipation of the next animal to be spotted. I stood on my seat in the Rover and poked my head and shoulders out of the open top area and watched intently the amazing landscape filled with African wildlife. Our guides were quick to give us species names and interesting facts about the park's wildlife. We started the day seeing zebras, impalas, baboons, giraffes, wildebeest herds, guinea hens, elephants, a stork, vultures, and, of course, the dik-dik, for which our lodge the previous night was named. Our group also spied many birds and, finally, at the end of the day, three lions lounging in a dry riverbed and also in a nearby sausage tree. I would call the lions the headliner on any African safari, and their elusiveness made them more difficult to spot. I loved the look in their eyes. They seemed to make eye contact with us and yet appeared positively bored to tears. My guess is that they were thinking it would be nice to have me for lunch, a nice juicy 150-pound tender American woman. Just as I thought this, the lion who was watching me licked his chops.

It was dry there, but the landscape was beautiful, filled with baobab and acacia trees. The trees were very unique in their shape and lack of leafiness, but we did see palm trees as well. At one rest stop, you could look down on the riverbed and see a troop of baboons in the river or other groups of animals making their way to water. But, the day's highlight was an up close and personal visit with several elephants within 10 feet of the Rover. I watched them as they gathered grass and munched happily while cameras snapped wildly; their eyes showed no fear of us. I was told that a full-grown bull weighs up to 6 tons, meaning that with one flip of his trunk, he could have sent us rolling in our measly 2-ton vehicle. Near dusk around 7 p.m., we headed toward camp and "deluxe camping accommodations" according to the brochure. The guides did not disappoint, as a large mess tent had been erected, where we had a delightful dinner and animated conversation. We learned a lot about the Masai culture, relationships, and traditions from our two main male guides, who both happened to be very interested in finding wives! The conversation centered in Godfrey's search for a wife and Ellie's search for a possible second. I guess in that part of the world, men were not limited to just one wife. I wondered whether he was sizing us up for possible contenders. The chatting continued, and the food was excellent, especially the vegetable soup. The only problem proved to be some ants that found their way into the butter jar on the table. The after-dinner campfire and starry night were the exclamation point to an incredible day. I retired to my deluxe tent, where a candle was lit on a stand and a sleeping bag and pillow were turned down on a cot. Camping on this trek was British Colonial style, and at no time did we have to lug gear or actually set up a tent.

Day 4: Sunday, "The Crested Breast"

We saw hundreds of birds on safari, but one especially stands out in my memory. The lilac crested roller is a very rare find, but with Ellie's help, we spotted it. We had a bit of trouble understanding the name.

Somehow between his translation, his Masai accent, and the hum of the Rover's engine, we were not sure whether we heard "lilac crested roller" or "crested breast." Someone even heard "chicken breast." In any case, it created loads of laughter. It got a little silly as the group laughed at the name of this bird, and I added fuel to the fire by announcing to Theresa, "My breasts have also crested," which sent us both into another burst of laughter until tears coursed down my face. We saw many species of birds and animals that day, but none was as memorable as the lilac crested roller and its newly discovered cousin the "crested breast." There always seemed to be something to laugh about, and the Tarangire was no exception. I think lack of sleep may have contributed to my demeanor that afternoon. As the laughter faded, we began catching glimpses of some new animals. That day, we saw the cape buffalo (whose horns made them look as though they were wearing old English wigs) and three or more species of eagles, waterbucks, many more colorful birds, a hyrax, an ostrich, a vervet monkey, more baboons, and, of course, elephants–hundreds of them. Also we saw a warthog, whose picture I was not able to capture. We spied a poisonous snake called the puff adder and some lizardlike creatures scrambling and sunning themselves on the rocks. I am so thankful that I had my journal to record as many species as I could. Without it, I fear I would have forgotten many. We ate lunch on a ridge that overlooked a swamp where hundreds of elephants could be seen bathing. I decided that this photo moment was the reason for a panoramic option on your camera. While elephants bathed and trudged through the swamp and riverbed, a mountain loomed in the background with an assortment of colors: pinks, yellows, and a deep green closest to us in the plains beyond the swamp. Other animal sightings that day included a hartebeest, which we saw for the first time, and many more whose names I cannot remember (nor could I write fast enough to record them all). After many hours, we drove back to "Camp Buffalo" for a shower and some dinner.

During shower time, I awoke from a nap to find Theresa running wildly about the tent and thrashing at something in the air. It turned out to be some angry African bees that had been attracted to her fruity, pear-scented soap she used during her shower. The showers were open air inside a tent, with large water packs heated during the day's sun. She quickly put away the scented body wash and toweled off while nervously scanning above her head for more buzzing insects. My shower was much less eventful, thankfully, and I enjoyed the warm stream of water and soap. Then I dressed and met our group for dinner. We once again engaged in some lively conversation with our guides, Ellie, Richard, and Godfrey, around a campfire. Deluxe camping turned out not to be a farce; we were very pampered and overconvenienced by our guides. Each night at dinner, they would prepare a soup that was unlike any other, and I only wish I could detail the taste or the ingredients for you. As I took out my pen and journal, I noted other safari game drive notables for the day: Theresa had proven to be quite adept at spotting giraffes. No matter whether they were 500 yards away or next to the road behind a tree, she always saw them first and would point them out to the group. Also, we seemed to be making inroads with some members of our group and feeling more comfortable with our new friends. Theresa and I were quite pleased at how we looked in our safari gear and hat, and, of course, the same rules apply in Africa as anywhere: "First you must look good before you succeed at any task," including grabbing binoculars for game spotting. Denny, the resident photographer, had taken a liking to us and regularly made us pose in his shots. I think we may have been his favorite subjects. Perhaps in his journal he recorded the species femalious gorgeous and wrote copious notes on our behavior.

Day 5: Monday, Jambo or Tomba?

Promptly at 7 a.m., our group breakfasted at Buffalo Camp, and then we drove out of Tarangire and headed to Lake Manyara National Park.

The road was incredibly bumpy, but the scenery made me forget all the jostling. We passed several Masai villages and saw the colorful locals who walked along the roads we traveled. Everyone wore bright reds, oranges, and yellows mixed together in patterns to form togalike clothing that draped around men's and women's frames alike. We passed children who ran along side the Land Rover and made motions to us, predominately with their hand holding a writing instrument and imploring our help. Godfrey explained that they wanted pens or pencils from us, but he encouraged our driver to continue on. He very simply asked that we not give any children or locals specific items, saying that it created jealousy and tension within groups of children. To him it was best that the Masai locals live with what their gods had provided them naturally on the land where they lived. He continued to explain Masai traditions and culture as we drove. I also noted with curiosity that some young teenage boys wore black clothing with ostrich feathers and had painted their faces white. Godfrey explained their appearance as part of the tradition for boys growing into manhood, and also during this time, they experienced circumcision and healing.

The entrance to Manyara was very unique and much greener than Tarangire, with many swift streams running through it. At the beginning of the day's game drive, a dense forest presented itself with many new species of tree we had not seen. Right away, we were able to get a close-up view of some very sociable baboons and their grooming rituals and mating and feeding habits. I watched as baby baboons hitched a ride on their moms' backs, which was a very adorable showing of closeness and baboon family customs. They were not shy, so we did witness a male baboon getting frisky with his female counterpart. Our guides informed us that you can tell a female baboon is in heat by the pink color of her bottom.

That day, in our vehicle, Godfrey was our day leader (Ellie was in previous days), and he was a very talented and fun narrator. We had decided the previous night at the campfire that Eddy Murphy would play him in the movies and Denzel Washington would play Ellie. After laughing at our comments, Godfrey pointed out animals as we drove slowly through. We stopped for a bit on the edge of Lake Manyara, a very large salt lake, and walked a bit down the shore to stretch our legs. Just after, a blue monkey made its first appearance, along with a marabou stork, near the lake's picnic area. The stork was one of the largest birds that I have ever seen, and it seemed like a flying pterodactyl in size, though its flight was quite smooth with its large wingspan. At lunch, we were entertained by a resilient baboon that could remove the lid and two rocks from a garbage pit cover and then disappear down below to collect leftovers. It actually put the cover back on when it had its fill. But, the highlight in Manyara was the many giraffes that we saw at quite close range. I marveled as they ate branches and leaves from thorned trees that dominated this park. As the giraffes ate from these trees, many times I ducked to avoid getting swiped by the thorned tree branches as they swept over the top of our viewing point atop the Rover. Manyara proved to be a smaller park but filled with amazing up-close game viewing of baboons and giraffes. As we left Manyara and the park's visitor center around 3 p.m., we learned some interesting Swahili words and terms during the ride:

Jambo	Hello
Jakoula njuri	Good food
Azuri	Awesome
Jakoula mjuri	Beautiful woman
Tomba	To have sex
Caribo	Thank you
Safe sana	Cool
Marvee	Let's go (Godfrey used this term often to tell the driver to go)
Marvy	Feces or shit (this term is similar looking to the above yet pronounced quite differently)
Akuna ma tata	"You have no butt" or "no worries," "no problem"

Jamba vs. jambo   The first passing gas; the second a greeting or "hello"

For any traveler abroad, you are no doubt familiar with language barriers that occur during your time in a foreign country. Some handle this barrier better than others. One of the members of our group, Linda, quite often would confuse the words she had learned. For example, when buying a postcard at a park visitor center, she said tomba instead of jambo, so you can imagine the clerk's surprise. Perhaps she was thinking about the famous Italian skier Tomba? One day later, she greeted a porter with Jamba instead Jambo, which made me laugh. The thought of her passing someone on a trail and nodding or smiling an acknowledgement while saying, "Did you pass some gas?" made me giggle.

While Theresa and I laughed about Linda's grasp of the new language, we headed to the Ngorongoro Crater. This famous African park is an ancient base of an old volcano that had formed a natural haven for animals over time. I had an incredibly difficult time saying "Ngorongoro" and kept butchering its pronunciation until asking our guides to say it several times for me. To say it correctly, you think of it as three parts: N-goron-goro. The crater and the roads had gotten progressively worse, but our driver, Richard, rifled down the rutted roads at 40–45 kph. My stomach began to feel a bit queasy that day, and it did not help that I picked the seat in the back. I slid open a window to catch some fresh air but succeeded only in letting in a squall of red dust that settled nicely in my hair and clothes for the rest of the drive. But we finally rolled by the gates and drove to the top of the rim at about 8,000 feet, where we all snapped some photos of this famous African vista. I could see the whole crater (some 7 miles wide) and its floor and lakes, reminiscent of the Grand Canyon but much flatter at its base. We continued on to the Serena Ngorongoro Lodge, a four-star resort with immaculate grounds and a nursery surrounding the lodge and rooms. It looked completely hand-crafted by masons, with round stones and mortar built into the side of the crater. My room had a view of the crater and a private deck. An African landscape and views are like none other, and I was captivated by the unique view of Ngorongoro at dusk. I pulled myself away from my lounge chair, and after a freshen-up from road dust, I joined the group for dinner in the main lodge, where our group was treated to a traditional Masai dance just before. Once again, the food was excellent, and Theresa and I let Godfrey tell us about his trip to the states for three months and his experiences on his "American safari." We had also been teaching Godfrey American slang. Earlier in the day, he had described giraffe fighting as "necking." I explained that "necking" meant something similar but different in English, something that might take place in the backseat of a car, at the end of date. We also taught him more modern versions of the word "necking," such as "kissing," "mashing," "making out," and even "the mash and dash," which was very amusing to him, and we all smiled at this vocabulary lesson.

Day 6: Tuesday, Ngorongoro Crater

My stomach was a little pissed at me on that morning, I think as a result of some exotic African spice from the previous night's dinner. So, Tuesday's start was a little shaky, plus the "tribe" made me get up at 6 a.m. for a 6:30 breakfast. Ughhh. I felt like I had an alien swimming around in my stomach, and I became a travel statistic. One-third of travelers will experience some type of stomach/digestive issues while traveling abroad. My sour stomach lasted through the morning as we made our way slowly down inside the crater. At about 8:30, we spotted a cheetah and, shortly after, two lions. I forgot my stomach ailments at that point and leaned out from my vantage point to get a closer look. The two female lions walked up the road toward us and passed right by the Rover, within feet of our vehicle. The two lions were so calm, and, conversely, we all whispered wildly about how close they had come to us. We watched the lions for what seemed liked hours. The two females parked themselves on a riverbank, with their paws stretched out in a very leisurely fashion. I learned that they do most of their hunting by night, so during the day, they lounged and waited for nightfall. Again, I was mesmerized by the casual look of their eyes watching us in amusement.

Once down in the crater, the floor itself was very flat, with a large soda lake in its midst. The rim was formed years ago when the volcano collapsed, so to get inside the crater, you enter via a road that "switched back" from top to bottom. The crater proved to be the place to see lions, cheetahs, hippos, flamingos, hyenas, and so much more. Our group also caught a glimpse of the very rare black rhino (there are only 30 known remaining). That day, we spent our lunch hour overlooking a hippo pool. At least three hippos took turns rolling and turning in thick mud, and one gave us a treat when it opened its mouth wide as if yawning and then plunged back into the depths of the pool of mud. After the hippo show, I took a catnap, with my head resting on a rock, and became the subject of some photos and laughter, unbeknownst to me while I lay snoozing. I ate a PBJ for lunch and downed a Sprite in hopes of calming my tumultuous stomach. We were able to take some great pictures with herds of wildebeests and zebras as a backdrop. While we were doing this, our driver took off unexpectedly, and Theresa's hat flew off, which we drove back for, grabbed, and dusted off.

As we left the crater that afternoon, we continued our cultural lesson, where we visited a traditional Masai village in the Ngorongoro Crater Conservation Area. We all gladly paid $10 for a tour of the village, which included a traditional Masai dance and a tour of one of the tribe's elders' homes—well, OK, actually, it was a hut. We followed Godfrey in through a very small opening, almost igloolike, and we hunched down and made our way to the center, where a cooking fire burned and smoke drifted up to an opening near the top of the roof. The hut itself was made of branches and held together by a mud/cow dung concoction that served as siding for the hut. We sat cross-legged by the fire and asked questions, which Godfrey translated. The elder woman was an older grandmother with brightly colored clothing and an enormous amount of earrings in not only her ears but also her nose and other parts of her face. She asked the women in our group (Theresa, me, Linda, and Alice) whether we were married, and, with Godfrey's help, we learned that she had more than 75 grandchildren. She was very intrigued that Theresa's family had 50 Black Angus cattle back in Michigan. In their culture, the number of animals or stock is directly related to status and wealth. Some people in our group traded with people of the village, things such as flashlights for handmade jewelry. It was incredible to meet people with such a drastically different culture; it was a good way to reaffirm some perspective on your own life and how you fit into the world. The Masai people of this village were very simple and very happy, and I had a deep respect for their way of life. Dirt floors, mud huts, no electricity, no modern appliances—just living off what the land and their animals provided them. It was hard to imagine what the Masai people would think of my family and friends, my condo, and our customs.

Day 7: Wednesday, "Tweener Day"

The safari part of our trip ended on Wednesday, and we loaded up the Rovers and headed out of Manyara Lodge back to Arusha and the Dik Dik Lodge. On the way, we stopped to shop at the Cultural Exchange. As I entered the facility, a woman danced with a mask while three men played African drums. Once inside, the store itself was an African version of a tourist trap, but there was still plenty to check out. Many life-sized carvings lined a small pool and garden area, and the other levels housed jewelry, smaller animal carvings, clothing, candles, and masks. Both Theresa and I found gifts for our families. We had them wrapped and then proceeded to the Internet café, where Theresa sent her sister an e-mail to say we were doing great and being treated quite well in wild Africa.

After lunch, our group headed to Dik Dik for a 4 p.m. briefing and an equipment check for the Kilimanjaro climb, which would be the second half of our two-week trip. At our meeting, Godfrey went over our mountain itinerary, and he then came to each of our rooms and went through a checklist. I barely passed the equipment check and was told I needed a few additions, such as warmer gloves; I also got a warning that I could be in trouble without ankle-high waterproof boots. I remember packing my bag before I left for this trip and thinking it would be impossible to need really warm winter clothes, but my perception would change as I got above 15,000 feet. Both Theresa and I had packed hiking shoes instead of boots. Oops. So, I guess I was as ready as I could have been. I brought myself and a good attitude, with a little faith that I would reach the top at 19,500 feet with our group. I was getting excited to start our climb, but I had grown tired of the conversations of most of our group, who discussed at great length using the drug Diamox to help hiking at elevations. To be honest, I had not researched it before the trip, so if I summited, it would be all natural. We enjoyed dinner with the group at 7:30, and I think everyone felt a combination of excitement and nervousness to start the climb.

Day 8: Machame Route on Kilimanjaro

On our first day of hiking, our group started with hundreds of other eager hikers at 6,000 feet, where each person must sign in to enter the trailhead. The temperature was about 70 degrees that morning, which proved to be in stark contrast to the temperatures at the top days later. On our first day on the mountain, we hiked six or seven hours through the rain forest section, with many snack and water breaks mixed in. It was muddy, and we had many roots to meander through, but the surroundings were extremely green and lush. The day's hike was generally not too steep, just a gradual gain, with Godfrey leading the way at a pretty slow pace–which we would thank him for later. Theresa followed closely behind Godfrey; I came next and then all the others. The vegetation was mostly green and wet, but it did give way to mountain heather, where the vegetation changed quite dramatically to scrubbier trees and bushes with much less color. We readied for night 1 in a mountain tent with no shower after perspiring heavily on our trek earlier. Dinner was held in a fairly cramped mess tent, but, of course, the food was tasty as always. So far, everyone was doing well, and on Friday, we would continue up to 13,000 feet. I was very tired that evening, and I noted in my journal that I didn't feel much like writing.

Day 9: Shira Camp

I would enjoy a second night in a two-person tent again with no shower. But besides the smell, we all made it to 13,000 feet. The hike was steeper on the second day, with rocks and scree to deal with and nothing much green left to see. We wore our boots with gaiters to protect our ankles and to keep out rocks and dust. So far, Theresa and I were handling the climb, the pace, and the weather–and just battling a little rankness. The nights had gotten colder, to around 30–40 degrees, so getting up to pee became a bit chilly. It was an adventure in itself making your way to the latrine, or what I called the "zoo toilets." A mental battle raged each night in my mind as I tried to convince myself that I could hold it and fall asleep. I would hold it as long as I could to avoid the late-night chill in the open-air three-sided canvas outhouse with a toilet seat placed over a hole dug in the ground that we all shared. Have you ever waited in line for an outside toilet tent?

We arrived at camp that day at 1:00, so we spent the afternoon watching Gladiator on Theresa's DVD player in the mess tent. It was quite a sight to see all 10 of us sitting on the small three-pronged camp stools and craning to see a 5-inch portable DVD screen. I think our "tribe" was quite pleased to have Theresa on the island that day. My ticket to stay proved to be a hiking game on the way up the mountain, the celebrity name game. My travel games from my childhood came in handy. We all took turns naming as we trekked up and around boulders. Everyone got a bit mellower that afternoon as we tired, but we did get a glimpse of the peak through the mess tent window. Snow-covered peaks, here we come!

Day 10: Saturday

It was my third day on Kili, and at 8 a.m., we started up a rocky slope over mountain tundra to our highest point of the day at 14,800 feet. The day started well for me, but I crashed at lunch; I don't think I drank enough water. Nothing sounded good to me of our lunch offerings, and I felt like I might toss. Over the course of half an hour, I managed to eat only a cookie and a small piece of bread. Most everyone had headaches to some degree from the altitude, but mine included loss of appetite and slight nausea. Our guides told us that today we would "climb high and then sleep low," which meant that after reaching 14,800 feet, we would descend 2,000 feet to our camp for that night. This was all part of acclimating to the altitude. We arrived at our camp at 2:00 that afternoon, and I promptly took a "camp shower," which consisted of a small basin of hot water and a bar of soap. The sun came out while we washed, and from our vantage point, we could clearly see the snow-covered peak for the second time. I also took the remainder of my water and soap and shaved my legs, which had some lengthy growth over the past few days. I am quite sure some of the porters who glanced my way wondered why I would waste water on such an odd ritual.

Before dinner, Theresa had constructed a mountain version of lawn darts. We all took turns throwing stones into the bull's-eye area she had created. Susie won with a clutch toss right before dinner. No one had much of an appetite, and most complained of ailments including headache, diarrhea, loopiness, sleeplessness, and so on. Everyone to some degree was feeling the affects of our first day nearing 15,000 feet. The next day would be the hardest day for our whole crew. And to quote Gladiator from the previous evening, "strength and honor" would be needed from this point on. I had begun to lose track of time, what day it was, and so on. Our routine at camp was going to bed around

8:00 or 9:00 and trying to sleep and then getting up when the sun rose. Dinner was always early at 5:30 or 6:00 because any later and your hands would be too cold to hold utensils. The previous night, the temps ranged in the 40s, and that night they would be around freezing or below. I had been sleeping mummified in my sleeping bag to stay warm and praying I did not have to get up and use the zoo toilets. That night, before falling asleep, I made some word scrambles for my tent mate, Theresa, to keep her occupied. Writing in the journal had been a good way to stay focused and keep us entertained at night, by reading several days' entries. Though the nights were cold, and even with the symptoms of altitude, the scenery was beautiful, and each day as we climbed, we would look down on views that could be described only through some of the photos I took. As we had learned, Kilimanjaro is the tallest free-standing mountain in the world, and we were approaching its peak. It is also one of the world's seven tallest mountain summits. I said a quick prayer for strength for the coming day. In the days ahead, I learned that you will know your limits only when you test them.

Days 11 and 12: Approaching the Summit

On Sunday morning, we awoke bright and early, as usual, to depart at 8 a.m. The routine was "wakey-wakey," as our porters said, at 6:30, with breakfast to follow at 7 a.m. There was never an opportunity for sleeping in on this vacation. The first part of Sunday was spent tackling "the Breakfast Wall." An 800-foot cliff loomed in front of us that had a narrow rock trail cut into it, basically a rocky switchback that was the most technical section so far. In one section of the wall, I had to skirt a rock protrusion with my back exposed to the river below. I took the opportunity to berate Theresa for talking me into this as I tried not to look down. In other sections, we took turns scrambling up steep 5–6-foot sections of rock and pulling each person up once he or she had a good foothold. For me, this was very nerve-racking since my primary fear in life is great heights. But, once at the top of the wall, I got a great picture of the clouds, which were now below us at under 14,000 feet. The day's hike was very long, and after the wall climb, we walked across a lunarlike landscape of shale and stone with no vegetation at all and then finally up a steep slope to Kili base camp at 15,200 feet. The peak was now clearly visible in great detail from our vantage point, and its snow-capped glacier glinted at me in the sun. Shortly after midnight, we would start the 4,500-foot climb to Uhuru Peak on Mount Kilimanjaro. There was a very good reason for starting the summit climb in the dark, which we would learn the next day. Apparently, walking in the dark for the first part of the summit helped to keep the mind focused on taking one step at a time versus continually watching the summit. That night for dinner in a very frigid tent, our group had all lost their appetites, and, in general, everyone looked a bit weary and potentially nauseous. For some unexplained reason, my appetite had returned, and I pounded down two bowls of a porridge-style oatmeal to the amazement of Theresa and the whole group. I was the first to lose my appetite but also the first to get it back.

Each day since we had started the climb, we'd hiked between four and eight hours per day. Godfrey had remained our main guide, with other assistants including Cambona, August, and Humphrey, who were all colorful locals. Olise and Francis also were assigned to Theresa and me, and each day, they cheerfully carried our luggage up the trail and then erected our tent and even made a stone patio at the entrance to our tent. Our group would start out each morning early, and the porters would stay behind and tear down and pack up the gear, and then, within an hour or two, they would stroll by us easily— some of them carrying up to 40 or 50 pounds balanced on their heads. They would smile easily and say Jambo as they passed. It did not seem that they were even breathing hard. I was positively amazed at their stamina and cheery disposition while carrying such heavy loads. Each day as we made it into camp, the porters would give us a high five and compliment us for making it so far. Francis and Olise would also bring each of us a small basin of hot water to wash up with before dinner. Literally, for each person on this trip, there were three porters or staff assigned to lugging gear, food, and water. By this time, even with the porters and pampering, camping had taken its toll on me, and I longed for a hot shower and the clean sheets of a bed. The adventure part was living up to expectation, but cramming in a pup tent each night became very aromatic, and, not to mention, the zoo toilets had taken on new heights. At dinner, Godfrey did his usual briefing for the next day's hike–summit day! I continued to listen to my travel mates obsess about taking Diamox. I thought to myself, "God, just shut up take the damn pill," and I leaned over to complain to Theresa as well. If you are sensing some hostility in my tone, you are quite perceptive, but I found out that altitude makes you think, do, and say things that you would not at sea level. I just felt weird and impatient, and the nagging headache made me testy as well. I had several "bitch attacks" while at altitude, one which happened in the morning when our porters came to our tent to offer coffee, tea or hot chocolate. In response to this kind offer, I sprang from my sleeping bag and yelled to Theresa to make them go away and that I didn't want anything! Of course, I was in a tent and they were well within earshot of my angry unfounded outburst. Theresa had to apologize to them on my behalf, with a nod that I would be fine and was just having a tough morning.

Godfrey told us that we would be woken at midnight and were to get dressed quickly and put on our headlamps for the ascent. But by then, it was only 6 p.m., and he told us all to get some rest, but my nerves prevailed, and I laid there for the four hours, all the while waiting with a monstrous rock under me on my side of the tent floor. At midnight, I heard the wake-up call, so I slid out of my sleeping bag and started layering for the cold. It was about 30 degrees but very windy. Theresa and I locked eyes for a moment as we layered up, as if to say, "Let's finish this." I pulled on a fleece, then a Windbreaker, and slid on my loaner gloves only to discover I had been given two left-handed gloves, so I pulled them on as best I could. Things started out fine, just my left hand looked like a mutant while I walked up the trail in the pitch black. The trail was very steep on this section, and all you could see was the small area in front of your feet that nine headlamps illuminated. The wind picked up about 20 minutes into the summit climb and proved to be very brutal the rest of the way. We encountered winds most of the way around 30 mph or gustier. The wind made the climb more challenging than we all would have liked. Our group put one foot in front of the other, or, in Swahili, "Polle, polle," said our guides to encourage us. After hours of slow trudging, because you couldn't move very fast with such small amounts of oxygen coming into your lungs, the group seemed to start to worry a bit about the cold. Michelle slipped and fell at one point, and I was struggling to keep my fingertips warm. Theresa was also freezing because of the wind, and as we passed 16,000 feet, my head was pounding right along with my heart. About halfway up the summit climb, I figured most everyone was wondering, "Why the hell did I pay to do this?" Two women in our group contemplated quitting and turning back, and I felt a bit dizzy; Theresa was no better, as her vision began to blur. During all of this, Theresa fell behind me 40–50 feet out of my sight, and I began to panic and wonder whether she was unable to continue for some reason. I could not imagine making it to the top without her, especially since she had talked me into the expedition in the first place. But somehow, we all plodded on, and at 6:30 a.m., we reached the rim of the crater near the summit. Through glazed-over eyes, I saw the sun come up over Africa. I would have attempted to take a picture if I could have moved my hands, but after some struggle, I realized my camera was frozen anyway. Godfrey took all of our cameras and placed them in his inner breast pocket to warm them up so we could try to get summit photos. The sunrise was an incredible sight but difficult to appreciate when you felt so awful. I was still dizzy from the altitude but kept going the last 500 feet to the summit, called Uhuru Peak. I felt as if I was veering left and right as I walked and could not quite keep a straight line. Theresa, meanwhile, battling being cold, stayed behind with Godfrey. Behind the shelter of a large boulder, she delayered in the bitter cold and added another fleece to try to hold in some body heat. Once she was redressed, they continued on and caught back up with the group. Near the summit, the wind and cold reached epic proportions. I have never felt cold like that before. Eight out of 10 of us reached the top, and we managed to snap a photo or two posed in front of the sign reading "Uhuru Peak," the tallest point in Africa at 5,895 meters. The group did not dally at the top, but the relief at reaching the top warmed me a bit. I noticed that after the photo, Theresa practically sprinted for the trail back down to camp. I took in the scene for a moment before descending. The mountain was an old volcano, so the rim over time converted itself into a glacier all around the perimeter. It was very beautiful, but did I mention cold? I can definitely say that this was the most physically and mentally challenging thing I have ever done. What a great story to tell, though, when I got back home–that I made it to the top of the tallest free-standing mountain in the world.

The walk down was a struggle at that pitch because of all the loose stones on the path. It was interesting to actually see the path I had walked up earlier in the dark just hours before. It was amazing how quickly your breath returned to your lungs as you descended even the first 1,000 feet. The sun came out, and it took about two hours for us to get back down to camp, except for Theresa, who had made it back down in record speed, using ski techniques slaloming down soft rocky areas of the trail. By the time I made it back with the group, she was curled up taking a nap in the tent. Most of us napped, too, and grabbed a bite for lunch since appetites were returning slowly. That day included seven to eight hours to the summit, then two to three hours back down to 15,000 feet, and at 3:00 that same afternoon, we set off again for another four hours to reach camp at 10,000 feet. My knees and hips were very sore at that point, as were my toes, from the constant pressure of walking downhill. My one walking stick was some help, but two would have been a better choice. Also, to my dismay, one of our travel companions, Linda, was transported past us resting on the shoulders of two guides who carried her down to camp. She had cramped earlier and was unable to reach the summit, so, apparently, she was given some special attention. I finally arrived at camp for the day and realized this would be my last night on the mountain and the fifth day without a shower.

Day 13: Tuesday

The sixth morning, we left Mweka camp in the morning and hiked down to 6,000 feet, where we were picked up and transported back to the lodge. The hike was about four to five hours through roots, hardened mud, and forest. On this last leg, we all chattered on about the experience, and Linda was especially energetic and peppy– probably because she herself did not hike the last four hours on her own two feet. So, she proudly set off in front of all of us, proclaiming how great she felt, which rustled a few feathers within the group. Not to be passed by a slacker, we picked up the pace, and Theresa very quickly passed her and put an end to her energetic banter and pace. I was glad to see that Linda was not the first to make it down to our checkout point. I was thinking as I walked, realizing that I had to go back home soon. I decided that the safari was my favorite part, but the hiking and camping on the mountain had taken their toll. I was so excited at the prospect of a shower and removing the stubble on my legs and the dirt from under my fingernails. At the bottom gate, you had to officially sign off the mountain. As we meandered toward our pickup, a crowd of people appeared at the bottom, consisting of many other groups returning and others preparing to go. Our porters were all waiting for us and very happily congratulated us on our summit. We took off some of our gear such as ankle gaiters and donated them to our porters, and I also left my walking stick behind. Our group made arrangements with Godfrey to tip our entire staff of guides and porters.

With many days of dust and grime on our skin, we loaded up thankfully and sped off toward the Dik Dik Lodge for our last supper with the group. As we drove back to the lodge, I looked back at Kili and had to laugh that we had just come off the summit the day before. I had also thought that any trip in my future would be lighter on the camping and roughing it side. I told Theresa that I got to choose the next destination. As I sat in the Rover, I realized how achy my legs and body were from the past six days. And, to make matters a bit worse, later that evening I would board a plane and endure the first of two eight-hour flights to return home. Finally, back at Dik Dik, we were escorted to rooms, where everyone scrambled to take their turn in the shower. I enjoyed that shower immensely and let the hot water run over me for a long time until I felt clean again. While we all showered and packed, our hosts had taken our hiking boots and washed and scrubbed them for us and had laid them out to dry on our porches. We all convened for one last meal and exchanged e-mails to share photos. I also watched a slideshow on Godfrey's laptop from someone who had been on a previous trip to Kili. Dr. Chip was his name, and I helped Godfrey compose an e-mail to him. I had noted that Dr. Chip was quite an attractive man! I told Godfrey to let him know I had made it to the top as well and that we had something in common. But, I could not linger too long, as most of us were booked on evening flights out of Arusha to Amsterdam. Godfrey shuttled us over to the airport, and we said our good-byes and waited in many lines to check bags and get boarding passes for the KLM flight. While we waited for boarding, Theresa sat in a lounge and charged her DVD player, and while she did this, an airport staffer swiped her bag of candy and chocolates that were to be our snacks on the plane. It was a sign of other bad things to come for her on this flight. We were seated in the middle of the plane, with an aisle in front of us, which I thought was cool because of all the extra legroom. Denny sat to my left, and we both tried to settle in and relax. This proved to be difficult, as people used our aisle as a freeway to head to the restroom or anywhere else on the plane. It was Theresa who took exception to the overuse of our aisleway and began blocking the path of passersby by stretching her legs out and resting them on the back of the seat in front of her. It was comical to see her stretched out and even more comical as people would approach and then lift their leg and swing it up and over her and continue right on through. We were also scolded by a flight attendant with a thick Dutch accent that we could not store our bags underneath our seats because of our seat placement. Theresa took great exception to this because her mp3 player was in her bag and she would not endure this flight without her tunes. There was no room in the overhead compartments, so Theresa and Helga haggled over a mutually agreeable spot for her backpack while Denny and I sat quietly, hoping the flight would get under way. Theresa sat down in her seat in a huff and stewed while the blushing attendant just kept saying "Everyting vill be OK." It was OK as we finally lifted off and things calmed down. We flew through the night to Amsterdam and then onto Detroit for the final leg of my airplane marathon.

Day 14: Flying Home

I arrived back in Grand Rapids on Wednesday afternoon, with a stop in the Netherlands and a few hours in the business-class lounge. My mind wandered, and I took in a USA Today newspaper and wondered what headlines I had missed. I also thought about a friend's wedding that I was in the coming weekend and wondered whether I would have fun with my date, Kevin. I didn't really think about work too much–that would have to wait until I could return to the ad agency and catch up with my coworkers. The time passed, and we boarded for the flight to Detroit, which seemed an endless eight hours, followed by much waiting to clear customs. Customs officials went through my bag and sanitized my hiking shoes and sprayed something on them before returning them to me. I was too tired to protest. Finally, we transferred to another terminal for the short flight to GR, where Theresa's mom was waiting to take us back home. Julie Hegedus gave us both a concerned look as we approached baggage claim. I am sure we looked haggard, with little sleep on the plane and not much time at all to recover from the summit hike. She also remarked that we looked thin, which I can believe after the long hikes and not feeling like eating on some days. She probably wanted to hear some stories, but I was mostly quiet on the 40-minute ride. I let Theresa and her mom catch up a bit in the car, and I rejoiced when we pulled in my drive and unloaded all my crap. I walked through my door and collapsed on my couch and closed my eyes for many hours.

People always ask me when I recount the Kili story, "Would you do it again?" My answer is always NO, once is definitely enough. I am very glad I did it; however, trust me, your answer would be the same after you came down from the summit as well. I am really glad I made the trip and could visit a new country so different from the United States. The one-week safari and the trek to climb Kilimanjaro in the span of two weeks, with no contact with family or work, were surreal. No phones, e-mail, or any contact at all made this trip truly more than a vacation but an experience I will not forget. The African wildlife, landscape, and people were so unique and devoid of any of the daily conveniences that I take for granted. For example, I view daily conveniences much differently now, such as flush toilets, pure drinking water, telephones, or computers, just to name a few things. I noted in my journal that the food was a nice surprise on the trip and Mountain Travel did a nice job to Westernize the palette but with plenty of authentic choices. Even so, my stomach was affected by all the new spices and flavors. The soups, on both the safari and the mountain, were incredible. They included tomato ginger, zucchini, cucumber, and many more. I also tried many things, such as ugali (the local staple), millet porridge (during the hike), avocado vinaigrette, and many sauces for rice and fish. Mint tea was also a staple, and it always seemed to help settle our stomachs.

Going without a shower for five days was also tough, so I had resorted to covering up my hair with bandanas or hats. Living out of a duffel and repacking a sleeping bag in a pup tent was trying at times and quite stinky. I was always up early, too, each morning because the group did not want to miss anything, especially the big cats in the Ngorongoro Crater. I seemed able to adapt and be flexible while working within the group's itinerary. During the camping, both Theresa and I came up with games to keep from becoming restless; you had a lot of time to think as you put one foot in front of the other while hiking each day. We walked a total of 37 miles on the Machame Route and drove hundreds of miles on bumpy and very dusty African roads. I was curious to see what other group trips adventure travel outfitters offer, but I knew I would be paying for this trip for a while, so I thought that I had better start saving then. A pretty "wild" trip, I thought, especially for my first adventure destination.

Photo left: Laura and Theresa freezing to death at the top of Kilimanjaro. Photos top to bottom: A visit to a traditional Masai village near the Ngorongoro Crater; A very rare hippo sighting; The elephants outweighed our vehicles by 3 tons each; A mere 20 feet away from 2 magnificent Lions on safari.

CHAPTER 3

Back to My Roots
Arizona, USA: March 15–20, 2002

In preparation for this trip, I made the three-hour drive from my home to Chicago and stayed with my sister, Charla, who lived in Wrigleyville, about two blocks from Wrigley Field. The next morning, with both of us hauling suitcases on rollers, we set off walking to the train that would connect us to O'Hare for a flight out. In hindsight, a cab ride would have been easier than walking briskly to the El and hauling a suitcase through tight areas and up and down escalators and then to our gate.

Charla and I were set to arrive in Tucson at 9:45 a.m. local time, where I knew my mom, dad, and brother, Ben, were eagerly awaiting our arrival. During the flight, I smiled as I flashed back to the many family trips that I had taken when I was much younger. The Holmes family tradition would now continue, as we were successful this year in gathering all five of us to spend a week together. We touched down and found our way through the airport and to baggage claim, where Mom, Dad, and Ben were waiting near our rental car, a white Buick. I laughed, as it took some serious cramming to fit all the bags (golf clubs, too) and five of us into this vehicle—just like old times. I felt 14 again and thought we might have to strap golf clubs on top of the roof like we had done in the past with bikes on top of the camper. I had hoped we could have graduated to a van or SUV to spread out, but I guess not.

As we piled into the Buick and I squeezed in the backseat next to the window, I sighed and realized that it had been a very long week at work while I was getting ready to leave. I hadn't had much sleep, but I noted to myself that I had a whole week to catch up. My dad had

41

booked a room at the Holiday Inn Express for one night because we could not check into the condo at the WorldMark Resort until Saturday at noon. The room at the "holly rock" was every bit as cramped as the car was, but we made it work for one night. Ben, Charla, and I propped ourselves up on pillows and got caught up on the March Madness basketball games. We had all entered in a pool by filling out a bracket sheet; Charla lead with 27 points, me with 25, and Ben with 20. We all chatted about plans and hikes we could take, and, of course, my dad wanted to fit in a round or two of golf as well. My eyes started to get heavy; I was tired but also very restless for the morning to come. I was in this new and exciting place and had not had a chance to see it yet, since we had driven to the area in the dark.

At the first peep of sun, my dad, true to his early-morning nature, was up and raring to go. The curtains were spread wide to reveal a vast blue sky with the burning sun ready to start its day. This may not be a big deal for some to see the sun in a totally cloudless blue sky, but for a west Michigan resident after a long winter, spring sunshine truly is an awesome sight. Living near Lake Michigan guarantees predominant cloudiness, especially in winter, and you can go weeks without seeing the sun. As a result, I was a victim of seasonal affective disorder (SAD), but I knew Arizona would cure my ailments quickly. I got up from my bed, rubbed my eyes, and sleepily followed everyone down the hall for a marginal continental breakfast and some weak coffee. After checking out of the hotel, we began again the arduous process of repacking the Buick and all its contents. We finally got moving for the short drive to the resort, and I got a chance to check out the desert terrain from the backseat again. Cacti dominated the landscape, and the Santa Catalina Mountains were to my right: majestic and pretty big but not snow capped like Kilimanjaro or the Rockies. The mountains in Arizona had their own earthy Southwest personality and were colored with hues of brown and pink. The sun left shadows on the eastern sides, which gave each range its own character and depth. The area around Tucson is primarily desert, and it is one of the sunniest cities in the United States, averaging 350 days per year. The annual rainfall is only 11 inches per year. In stark contrast, western Michigan receives, on average, more than 100 inches of snow each year. Anyway, I was glad to be there, and the odds were good that we would see the sun every day we were there.

Once at the WorldMark, my mom ran off to do some grocery shopping nearby as Charla and I quickly donned swimsuits to absorb some much-needed rays. Ben and my dad ran around on the tennis court for an hour and then joined us poolside. It was a bit cloudy, but the sun came out in force by the afternoon, and temperatures hit the high 60s. The locals said it was a bit chilly, but it seemed tropical to us Northerners. Charla and I gave up sunbathing in the early afternoon as a big cumulous cloud rolled in, which Ben said was the first cloud he had seen since Tuesday. We walked back to the condo to unload and unpack and grab a bite to eat. The accommodations were very nice, and we had a spacious two-bedroom adobe-stucco building, very much like every other condo or home. The architecture did not seem to vary much except by color, but it seemed to fit into the landscape quite well. Our patio and yard were a nice red rock mixture with vegetation that required little or no water and provided a great vista out toward the Catalinas.

After reading a barrage of tourist guides, we settled on a drive to Sabino Canyon around 3:00 and planned a hike to Seven Falls in Bear Canyon. The visitor center operated two trams, one a narrated tour where lazy types could enjoy the scenery without any walking and the other that took you on a short ride to a trailhead where you embarked on a 2.6-mile journey to the falls at its end. Of course, I chose the latter, but my mom opted for the lazy train, as she was still bothered by a sore back. Ben, Charla, Dad, and I, with a pack and some water in tow, started up the trail at about 4:15. We got a warning from the tram driver that we were getting a late start and may encounter dark on the way back. We assured the driver that we were quick and could handle it, and

I casually mentioned that I just recently climbed Mount Kilimanjaro—and suppressed a wink while I said it. So, off we went at a military pace up a gradual slope. The trail featured seven crossings of a river, with big boulders for stepping-stones. As we walked deeper into the canyon, the sides rose up higher around us and enclosed us. Some were sheer cliffs in sections, and once we reached the final crossing, we started up a 600-foot climb of switchbacks. We stopped for some photos, and Ben even managed to make it in a shot using the timer, despite a 10-yard sprint and a quick leap onto the boulder with us. The trail switched back to its highest point and then immediately back down to the base of the falls and cut into the rocks. Not much water was actually falling down the rocks, but there were several tiers of pools that gave way to the next level of smaller, flatter areas with small pools. Ben let out a big yell to check the echo factor in the canyon, and it also served as the signal to head back. We had to navigate an hour back on the trail and then another hour on the dirt road back to the car because the trams stopped running at dusk. It was an easy hike by most standards, but we had set a very quick pace to avoid hiking in the dark. Charla made it back in first, having run part of the way. I followed next, unable to keep up with her, and Ben and my dad brought up the rear. Tired and hungry, we collected my mom, who had waited for us in the visitor center parking lot and set off to find Gentle Ben's Brewery next to the University of Arizona. After a couple of wrong turns, we finally arrived and ordered some burgers and home brews. Ben enjoyed two frothy Copperheads, and I downed two cold and light Tucson Blonds—yummy. I fell asleep in the car on the way back and didn't even make it past 10 p.m. I was still apparently on Michigan time.

Sunday, March 17

I woke up the next morning to a view of nothing but blue sky, and it made me smile. I got up and sat on the patio and enjoyed the view of the distant mountains and the warmth of the sun. By 9:30, we had showered and dressed and found a community church just down the road. There was no skipping church on our family vacations. We arrived and congregated with a nice group of retirees, who all gave us a hearty handshake and thanked us for visiting. As I looked around, seated in a traditional wood pew, I noted that my mom and dad, who were in their midfifties, were at least 20 years separated from the median age range of these churchgoers. We hymned and listened to a well-articulated sermon, said our good-byes, and headed back to poolside sunning.

I inhaled my lunch so as not to miss any sun time, which was silly since it never seemed to disappear behind any clouds in Arizona. Only in Michigan do you feel compelled to scramble outside to soak up rays for the mere moments the sun shows itself sometimes in winter or spring. The sun felt incredible, and I was delighted when I pushed my bikini strap aside to find a tan line within a half hour. But, I could lounge only so long, and so Ben, my dad, and I left Charla and Mom poolside and headed to the golf club at Vistoso for a 3:00 tee time. Arizona golf courses are unique and the opposite of Michigan's lush green grass and fairways, of course only in season. Here, the tee boxes were like sections of green carpet, magically transported and set amid the desert. I was not used to seeing much vegetation in the area that was a deep velvety green, so it made being on a golf course seem incredibly lush when surrounded by cacti and sand. My brother worked his magic with the golf pro at Vistoso, where he played his "professional courtesy" card and got us on the course for only $25 (the rate card was $150). At the time, Ben was working as an assistant pro at a private club near Dana Point, California, called Marbella, so he was always good to have around when it came time to play golf. Anyway, desert courses are challenging because the rough (what I would normally call tall grass or the woods) is made up of cacti and a plethora of plants with sharp, pokey protrusions. If you hit your ball off course, I'd suggest you take the penalty and move on. Vistoso also featured double fairways, where you hit over one desert area onto a landing area, only to do it again to reach the green. I was quite pleased with a 53 on the front nine, which featured a couple 200-yard drives for me and a pretty consistent 3 wood. I did have a significant problem on a par 3 when I landed in a pot bunker and three shots later I still was not out. An 8 on par 3 will piss anybody off, and because of my dawdling in the sand, the sun had started to set, so we did not complete a full 18. As we loaded up the clubs, the sun turned the Catalinas pink for a few minutes until it went down and they returned to their original earthy brown. The mountains seemed warmer and less menacing in Arizona, perhaps because no snow graced the peaks and the colors were softer. My dad thought that they looked inviting and peaceful. I had worked up an appetite as I watched the last drops of sun disappear from the sky. The three of us returned to the condo and had dinner: steaks on the grill washed down with some Beaulieu Merlot.

Monday, March 18

The weather was very brisk by Arizona standards, so we decided to pack a cooler and do some exploring to the south of us. This meant that the five of us would have to climb in the Buick again. So, I volunteered to drive, which meant more legroom and control of the music. At 9:30, we hit the road heading south of Tucson, toward Benson, and then to Tombstone, home of the OK Corral and many famous Western movie sets. I drove for 10 miles at a time and passed nothing but tundra–no houses, just what seemed like an endless loop that kept repeating itself: such was southern Arizona by car. Tombstone was a tourist trap, so we quickly bypassed it and continued south to my birthplace down highway 82 to Sierra Vista. Charla called it Sierra Nevada instead, like the beer. This would be my first return trip to my birthplace. Just outside of Sierra Vista was Fort Huachuca the army base, where my mom and dad lived from 1966 to 1970. My dad was a sergeant and served as a mailman and dental supply specialist while stationed at the fort.

They lived in a flat-roofed hacienda on the base at the foothills of the Huachuca Mountains, and after driving around many neighborhoods, we were not sure whether we had found the old residence. They all looked the same to me.

We stopped first at the main gate and had to get a permit to enter, which gave us a chance to stretch our legs a bit. Once the permit was in hand, we drove to Raymond W. Bliss Hospital, where I was born. We took a few ceremonial pictures out front, me posing with Mom and Dad. I noted how small the hospital seemed—and I live in a pretty small community with a regional hospital. My dad remembered that a medical student (at best) delivered me some 32 years ago at Raymond W. Bliss, and my mom vividly recounted being admitted with labor pains and how her nurse had promptly sent her down to the cafeteria to eat! Well, somehow it had all worked out, and I arrived a fit and healthy army brat back in '69.

We got lost leaving the base but finally managed to find Highway 82 again and headed south to Nogales and the Mexican border. I was amazed at the level of activity at the border. There were lines of cars and people going into Mexico and even longer ones to return to the states. A heavy dose of panhandlers and beggars lined the street, and some walked in between rows of cars with signs saying they were primarily seeking food or money. We navigated through this mess and, after much searching, found a parking lot and set off to check for souvenirs at the open market areas. We all did some haggling with the locals and picked up some odds and ends or gifts. Dad chose a leather belt, Charla selected a small Mexican blanket, and I picked out the same, just a bit larger. My mom found a bracelet, some pottery, and also a rather ornate thimble. We would have stayed longer, but some shops were closing, and it was unseasonably chilly. Temps had fallen in the low 50s. Apparently, we had brought a bit of the North Country with us to the normally hot and dry Southwest.

Tuesday and Wednesday

The weather improved the next days, with a beautiful blue sky and perfect temps in the 70s, so Charla and I headed off to the pool area to bronze ourselves. We had the most sunbathing stamina, while Ben and my dad required an activity such as tennis or playing in the pool. I was content to read and just relax for a while and relish not being crammed into a car. We had arrived poolside about 10 a.m. and developed a system of rotation and flipping so as not to burn one side. I did play a bit of tennis with Ben to see whether I could still manage to hit it over the net with some frequency. My backhand sucked, so I spent a lot of time trying to get in position to use my forehand. Half an hour was all I mustered, but after calling tennis quits, my family and I packed a bag to do another hike at the nearby Catalina State Park. This time the five of us set out on a two-mile loop on Romera Canyon Trail. The trail wound us through the foothills of the Catalinas and was lined with saguaro and prickly pear cacti. We took lots of pictures with them as the backdrop, and it reminded me of taking pictures in Africa on safari, where the zebras were as plentiful as the cacti were on our hike. Ben managed to lean into a cactus during a photo, so Charla and I took a moment to remove a few spikes from his back. I had received my "cactus bite" earlier in the week on the golf course. The trail continued up, and Ben, Charla, and I had put some distance between us and Mom and Dad, who had stayed behind at a slower pace. We followed a ridge up to check out Romera Canyon. The trail description had promised some water or pools at the top, but they were nonexistent since it had been so dry in the area. We headed back down and caught up to my mom and dad and took a short ride back to shower and clean up for dinner. We drove down the main street in town, as most tourists do in the area, and found an authentic Mexican restaurant called La Parilla Suiza. Charla thought it was a version of a Mexican Denny's, with its casual cantina atmosphere complete with plastic tablecloths and paper placemats. I didn't care, and it seemed just right to me once the hot salsa and pico de gallo arrived. It seemed a far cry from Denny's as we ordered a feast of enchiladas, shrimp, and more. The margaritas on the rocks were quite good, and I could have dined on just those and the chips and salsa. Having gorged on dinner, I rolled back to the condo and took in a bit of television before retiring to the bedroom that I shared with my sister.

Another sunny day greeted me the next morning–what a surprise! I really was delighted to forget all the gray days I had endured during my Michigan winter. Each day it had gotten progressively warmer, and that day was forecasted in the low 80s, and Thursday was projected to hit 91 degrees. I spent the morning in the sun, as was the routine, but I fit in some tennis again to get my heart rate up a bit. I improved from my earlier attempt and made a game of it for a while, with Ben serving as my net mate.

It was too hot to be in the sun all day, so my mom had taken to searching for activities for us in the plethora of tourist magazines she had collected from the resort lobby area. She selected a day trip to downtown Tucson and the Fourth Street area. There was a bustling downtown area with blocks of shopping brimming with Southwest-flavored gifts and many bars and lounges serving Corona, Tecate, and other regional favorites. We meandered through a few stores and picked up some trinkets that we felt were a good representation of Tucson and Southwest style. I grew weary of shopping and suggested we stop in at O'Malleys Sports Bar and Irish Pub for some sustenance before heading to the baseball game–Diamondbacks vs. Padres. My dad has always been a baseball fan, primarily during the Detroit Tigers' run in the '80s, but we thought it would be nice to take in a game on this trip with the whole family. At O'Malleys, I enjoyed two tall Tecates with a lime wedge garnish, and I would venture to say they tasted much better than their close relative, Corona. While I collected our tab, my brother and dad had ventured off and secured the Buick and pulled it up in front of O'Malleys so we could get moving to the baseball game. With a late start, we encountered some traffic issues along the way, which made us late for the game and caused us to miss the national anthem. We collected some junk food on the way to our seats, which were on the first baseline about 15 rows up. We watched nine innings of the hometown D-Backs in the Randy Johnson era vs. the Padres, which ended in a 4-4 tie. Baseball games can be eternally boring, so we filled our time with bags of popcorn and peanuts–anything to keep us busy while we watched and waited. Now I know why baseball players are constantly spitting, chewing, or blowing bubbles: they are just as bored as the fans are in some cases. We also took part in a lively rendition of "Take Me out to the Ballgame," and we longed for some foul ball action to liven up the lengthy game. We did have a very animated local super fan sitting in front of us, who yapped incessantly about her D-Backs and how awesome they were. Ben made conversation with her, and he slipped in that the uniforms were ugly, no matter how good the team was. She was good-spirited about the comment and probably fired back about how bad the Tigers sucked. More animated cheering came from her section, but Ben did manage to get a suggestion from her for dinner and libations. She suggested we belly up at Famous Sam's, a sports bar in Oro Valley, and not miss the University of Arizona wildcats basketball team, who played Thursday at 6 p.m. I liked the idea of hanging out a local establishment while cheering for the hometown Cats. The drive home was nice, and I watched the clear sky and an abundance of stars from my window. After a bit of reading back at the condo, I fell quickly asleep. Many days in the sun, several in a row, take a lot out of you.

Thursday

At 9:30 a.m. the next morning, on my last day in sunny Arizona, I sat on the patio and attempted to read, but the sun was so intense I started sticking to my chair. It was around 75 degrees at that moment, on its way to 91 that afternoon. Our morning routine held true, and Charla, my mom, and I were poolside by 10:00 to put finishing touches on our golden tans. Ben and my dad usually found an activity and started bugging us around noon, ready to start that day's action. So, at lunch on most days, we ate sandwiches and had a family forum for our afternoon drive and sightseeing opportunities. It was decided by popular vote that we would make the drive to Mt. Lemmon, Arizona's only ski resort area. I managed to outmaneuver Ben and Charla for the driver's seat and smiled at my luck at not being in the backseat. I had had my share of heavy-footed acceleration and braking from my parents during the week. I think at age 50 something happens to drivers that renders their abilities behind the wheel less than optimal. We settled in for our final road trip past Sabino and into the foothills and then onto the Catalina Highway that takes you on a winding road up the mountain. As I guided us up the road, the scenery changed from saguaros and cacti to greener plants and evergreens, but the usual Southwest peculiar red rock formations dominated the scene. I called them "thimble rocks," with layers upon layers of stacked rock that rose up with a small base for all their height, defying gravity and looking as if they would fall off their perch at any moment. I would sometimes get the urge to think I could stand behind one and merely push it off its resting point. The drive was very scenic and reminded me of the Blue Ridge Parkway, with many switchbacks and a scenic pull-off about every half mile. I kept my eyes on the road since it was narrow and flanked by fallen rocks and steep cliffs.

We stopped at several vistas for photos and eventually made our way past 8,000 feet in elevation to the base of Ski Valley and Mt. Lemmon. Once at the resort, we found that the chair lift was running for tourists who wanted to pay for a ride to the top and a pretty view. We opted to walk around and stretch our legs and did a quick walk-through of the ski shop. There were still sections of snow in the shaded areas, where the sun's heat had not melted the last of Mt. Lemmon's base. It was a small ski hill by most standards, but it had the corner on the market in this state, as it had no other competition. It was weird to see any snow at all, but it was considerably cooler up at this elevation.

There really was not much to see, so we all became preoccupied with what we might eat for lunch and found a snack stand that sold us some fudge. Ben and Charla always seem to be constantly hungry, and they began rooting in the trunk in search of the cooler and its contents. We munched on some pasta salad and cheeses and then walked through Summer Haven and to a trailhead called Marshall's Gulch. We set off through the pines and ponderosa on a moderately elevated footpath, but we found that our breathing was more difficult at this elevation than it had been at only 3,000 feet. Luckily, the trail was very shaded and cool for the most part, but it did lead us out into the open to a ridge that held a huge solitary boulder that we climbed on and took in the noteworthy view. Ben continued on the trail with my dad, and Charla and I headed back on the trail to catch up to my mom, who had stayed behind to guard the Buick and our cooler. Charla and I took our time, so the guys eventually caught up to us. First came Ben, who motioned for us to be quiet and hid behind a mammoth pine and tried to scare my dad as he came down the trail. We all laughed and continued down the path, and the guys told us that when they had first started walking back, they swore they heard a wild animal growl or grunt twice. In any case, we picked up the pace and looked over our shoulders a few extra times but made it back without any sightings of the animal they heard.

We piled in the Buick and recounted our hike for my mom as we drove back down the way we had come, in search of a dinner spot. I was starving and realized that I always worked up an appetite after hiking. About an hour passed, and we arrived at the Great American Cattle Company, where we ordered burgers and Ben and I cold Pacificos, of course with a lime. We watched March Madness basketball on television, featuring Arizona vs. Oklahoma, and we also witnessed Indiana beat Duke (go Big 10)–we all cheered! None of us was very fond of Duke, so we rooted heavily for our Midwest neighbors, the Hoosiers. We finished our meals and headed back the WorldMark at Vistoso for a final soak in the hot tub. Later that night, we all took time to start packing up suitcases for our trip back the next day. As I thought about the week we had just spent, I smiled as I realized how many things had not changed on the Holmes family vacation, from now to over 20 years ago. There was still the same eagerness to see new sights; the long, arduous trips in a cramped car; and family picnics shared at a well-chosen scenic area or park. But, some things did change as we had all aged. Charla, Ben, and I did not pick fights in the backseat; instead, we "fought" for the wheel. And the most notable difference was that we no longer camped on our trips but secured accommodations in a well-appointed condo. I thought we were moving in the right direction.

Top photo: Siblings-Laura, Ben and Charla among the cactus.
Bottom photos left to right: Laura with her mom and dad in front of the hospital at Fort Huachuca where she was born; Charla posing by an "ass" shopping in Nogales, Mexico.

CHAPTER 4

A Wet One

Costa Rica, Central America–May 24–June 2, 2002

After reading and digesting many travel books and catalogs, I had decided a multisport adventure in Costa Rica would be my next destination. I was lured by photographs of the lush green rainforests and images of wild white water. I had never been to Central or South America, so it seemed a natural step to add this to my list of travels. And so far, traveling with an outfitter with a group of people had served me well in Africa, so I thought I would give it a try again. Of course, meeting a group of strangers at the beginning of any trip can be a bit worrisome, but my trusty travel companion, Theresa, whom I traveled with in Africa, was also on board for Costa Rica, so that eased my mind a bit about spending a week with total strangers. As with most trips, the planning, travel arrangements, and equipment list kept me busy in the months before departure. But, I do love those times leading up to an adventure and the anticipation and excitement that build; they really motivate me to work diligently at my day job so I will have the resources needed to keep traveling. As May 24 approached, the familiar buzz of excitement permeated my days, and finally we drove off toward Gerald R. Ford Airport in Grand Rapids, Michigan, where the journey began for me. The first day of any trip is always travel day, and this one started uneventfully at 10 a.m., when we flew down to Dallas and then onto San José, Costa Rica. We arrived around 9:30 p.m. local time and were greeted by a light, warm rain. After clearing security, we met up with the group.

Our guide on this trip, Alejo, was perched on the curb with a "Mountain Travel Sobek" sign in his hand. He had collected the other five members of our group; Theresa and I approached and exchanged greetings with our new friends. We met a father/daughter combo, Joe and Jennifer, and also Eileen and Jeff (husband and wife), who had also brought Jeff's dad, Jerry, along. Over the hum of voices and traffic, the group had a little trouble with my name, and Jerry proudly shook my hand and said, "Nice to meet you, Flora!" I smiled good-naturedly and corrected him, but I had quickly earned a nickname on the bus ride to our hotel. My Costa Rican pen name, quite appropriately, is Flora, which seemed a perfect name, considering our lush rain forest surroundings. We encountered more "name fun" during check-in at San Gildar, our hotel in San José that served as our home base. The group had all checked in, and we learned that our room was reserved under Laura Holmes and Thomas Hegedus instead of Theresa Hegedus. We all laughed, and I thought to myself, "I am on Flora and Thomas's excellent adventure." I was so excited to be in the tropics that the rain did not bother me, partly because the temperatures were in the 70s. San Gildar was a gem, and it boasted an open-air pool in the middle, while the rooms on two levels flanked all sides of it. Palm trees rose up around the pool, and all sorts of very green and leafy plants made their presence known. The rooms were simple but very nice, with tiled floors and painted warm colors on the walls. I noted that there were no mosquito nets as there were in Africa, but several species of bugs did make an appearance to welcome us. The bugs' visit gave us the quote of the day from "Thomas," my roommate. "Oh, my God, big-ass beetle on the floor!!" she exclaimed while unpacking some clothes. I laughed, and since it did not seem too menacing, I neatly pushed it out the door so it could bother someone else. Not to be outdone, a small wood spider also greeted me as I drew the shades, and it was at that time that I decided a "bed check" was necessary before climbing into the sheets. I threw back the covers, and to my relief, there were no bugs in my bed. Thank goodness. Alejo had encouraged us to get some sleep because a 4:30 a.m. wake-up call was in store to get us moving on a long drive the next morning. So, I laid out some clothes and promptly fell asleep.

The activities and conditions of the next few days made it very difficult to keep track of things in my journal, and I found myself writing three days' worth of events after the fact. The quote in my journal read, "Author's Note: I am writing this after three days and two nights at the beach camp or 'playa casera' of which it DID NOT RAIN a total of 5 hours the entire time we were there." The surroundings were beautiful and secluded, with the whitest sand I had ever seen, but when waterlogged, you see things with different eyes. In more than 15 years, Alejo said he had never seen it rain that much! He mentioned that it usually rained a total of two hours within the scope of three days! Not so on this excursion. The adventure took a turn, and on what was supposed to be our third night at beach camp, we were forced to "abandon ship" and hike out back to Curu Refuge. A tropical depression and high tide rolled into our camp and drenched the mess tent and swamped most of the sleeping tents as well. The surf was almost successful in taking our kayaks out to sea, until all of us and our guides furiously fought the waves to pull them farther into shore and out of reach.

So, let me "backpaddle" to Saturday morning and describe the events of my first rainy three days in Costa Rica. Saturday started with much promise but a bit early for my liking (5 a.m.). The early-morning call came, and I dressed sleepy-eyed and joined our group in our van for our journey to the coast. The sun came out in force, and we headed west and north of San José on winding and very hilly roads dominated by rain forest and coffee fields growing on steep side hills. We took a midsized bus toward Puntarenas while winding through mango fields and coffee fields in elevations of 7,000–8,000 feet or more. Along the route, we stopped for a breakfast of eggs, rice, and black beans and, of course, coffee. At our stop, old remnants of sugar cane processing equipment were rusted but displayed nicely under a wooden canopy and picnic shelter. I learned how this equipment had aided in boiling and transferring the sugar cane en route to its final form of refined sugar. We drove on for an hour or so to a small town where we would catch a ferry to cross the Gulf of Nicoya to get to the Curu Refuge on the western side of Costa Rica. The sun was out, and it was quite hot as we perched on the front deck of the ferry and took in views of the panoramic gulf/inlet area. Intermittent showers came and went in short spurts on the ferry ride and continued with us as another bus brought us to our kayak send-off area. Both our guides, Alejo and Jimmy, gave our group a "Kayak 101" course, and we all had to pass a "flip test" before our group was cleared to paddle around the inlet. They described how if your kayak overturned, you should simply relax, not kick your legs inside the craft, and let yourself fall out of the kayak underwater and, then, once clear, come to the surface. As an example, Jimmy demonstrated. Alejo turned the kayak, and Jimmy quickly went under, but he popped out of the kayak skirt underwater and stood up in the chest-deep water. I had a little trouble on my flip test. I volunteered to go first so I could get it over with, but in my nervousness, I had misunderstood the directions and thought they would roll me back to the surface while I stayed in the kayak. Alejo flipped my kayak, and I tried to lean with its natural turn and rotation. I thought I would come back up on my left side—but I realized after several seconds that Alejo was not rolling me back up, so I needed to escape my watery craft and get to the surface. I am sure I had an exasperated and confused look on my face as I broke to the surface while sputtering and pushing my wet hair away from my eyes. I was a bit embarrassed, and Theresa gave me a look as if to say, "What the hell were you doing?" Everyone else in the group mastered the flip test without incident, no doubt inspired to do better after my initial try. I did master the rest of my sea-kayaking instructions and learned paddling techniques and how to steer and maneuver through surf and waves. Our group paddled out together in crystal blue seas with the sun on us for the moment, and we headed toward the beach camp that was to be our home for three days. The gulf water was warm, and it connected around the island to the Pacific Ocean. Warm showers greeted us again, but I did not mind, as I realized we were coming into an open beach area where I could see tents and a camp set up. Sea kayaking seemed pretty easy, but I learned that the difficult task with the long length of the vessel was starting out through surf and also landing and disembarking as you hit the beach. The force of the waves started to push you sideways, so you had to hurry and pull out of your kayak skirt and get your legs on land. I was trying to hop out of my kayak as I beached, and Aljeo caught me before I barrel-rolled into the frothy surf and sand. We pulled our kayaks up the beach, and once my feet were on solid ground, I took a look around.

The scene of our beach camp was just as you would see on an episode of Survivor, on a deserted beach near a remote tropical island. Two-person tents lined the beach perimeters. My tent mate, Theresa, selected a tent away from the main grouping and farther back from the beach area. This selection would prove to be most fortunate and immune to the high tide that plagued the other tents–but more on that later. We all stowed backpacks in our tents and gawked at our surroundings of palm trees, lush forest, seashells, and scurrying hermit crabs near the pounding waves. It was perfect–well, almost perfect. It began to rain and rain some more. The sunscreen we had searched for and bought near Puntarenas earlier would be of no use to us now. Instead of basking in the glow of evening sunset, we found ourselves stranded under a drooping mess tent with five strangers. Our evening was spent dashing between tents: the mess tent, the sleeping tent, and the toilet, which was not a tent but three uncovered side walls, by the way. Ahhh, the "zoo toilets" had reemerged in Costa Rica.

It would get wetter. We all ran to our tents Saturday night with hopeful optimism that the sun would shine on Sunday. A lovely damp scent had begun to permeate our tent, and Theresa began to place candles or linen water near her nose to combat the smell. In the early hours before we woke, the rain let up a bit, but as we prepped for kayaking, it began in earnest again. Soaked through, we paddled through tropical showers and headed for Tortuga Island about 1.5 miles away. We made it to the shores of Tortuga and beached our kayaks more gracefully than the day before. It was a bit chilly in our wet gear, so it actually helped to swim in the water, which was warmer than the air. Alejo gathered us, and we set off on a hike to the top of the island and learned some local flora and fauna and munched on fresh mango as we went. It was still raining. The mangos were handpicked by Jimmy, our 24-year-old superhot guide, who drew my gaze on more than one occasion. He was 5'9", with a deep tan and perfect flat stomach and spectacular pecs and shoulders, no doubt from paddling and lifting gear all the time. Anyway, I digress, but he was a bright spot in a few days of clouds and rain. Just take a look at my pictures and you'll see what I mean.

On the paddle back, Alejo led us through and between two islands with rocky outcroppings, where the waves were a bit rougher than in the open areas. Everyone made it through without using our "flip test" knowledge, but I noticed that Theresa was looking a bit green as we would rise and fall in huge oceanlike swells. We pressed on through large rolling waves and made it back to camp for lunch. Meals usually meant something wrapped in a soft flour tortilla, and today was a potato salad or tuna salad "burrito." The rain stayed with us, on and off again, and we made the best of it and swam in the waves with fins on and walked on the beach while keeping a lookout for tree or howler monkeys that lived in the area. Snorkeling was out because the constant rain had clouded the water and limited any underwater sightseeing. As we walked, we noted the two rocky areas that bordered each side of camp, and as they broke, the waves created the constant roar of water. Hermit crabs dotted the beach, and literally thousands of them scurried every which way as you walked. They patrolled the beach and ranged in size and color, with bright purples, pinks, and oranges covering their shells. We even had hermit crab races because we were marooned in the rain. Eileen, a member of our group, was bored after dinner and with Theresa set up races with two handpicked crabs with the help of her husband and father-in-law. We also discussed at great length that our skin and entire bodies were completely waterlogged and unable to dry and that this fact was causing some discomfort and itchiness. I even overheard Eileen tell her husband how bad her backside had begun to itch from sitting in wet kayak bottoms all day. I think we all had some version of adult diaper rash from our soggy adventures. Alejo tried to keep our spirits up by serving us happy-hour drinks each evening. One night was cervezas, then next tequila, and also sangria. I do think the alcohol helped put me to sleep as we listened to another evening of rain pounding our tent. As I lay there, I marveled at each drop and wondered how much longer our tent would remain waterproof. To combat the rain and the tent's damp floor, Theresa used her engineering background and dug small trenches around the perimeter of our tent, which funneled the water in tiny rivers away from the tent's bottom. It was a brilliant move and much needed as the rain and the wind kicked up for another night. I lay awake and was really quite scared that our tent was literally going to be picked up by the wind and blown down the beach with us inside it. In such a small space, the sound of the rain and wind was magnified, and I slept fitfully on and off until morning came.

Monday morning dawned, and, once again, the early-morning hours (from 5 to 8 a.m.) proved to be the only reprieve from the rain. Wake-up time was usually around 6 a.m., since we had all gone to bed early, tired, and bored around 9 p.m. For the second day in a row, we all paired up and shoved each other into the surf for more sea kayaking. Sea kayaks are incredibly buoyant and stable, as I found out that morning. The trick to launching a sea kayak is to paddle very hard through the first two waves of incoming surf and avoid getting hit by a breaking wave. As Alejo shoved me out into the surf, I paddled furiously as I saw an 8-footer coming fast; my hope was to get over the top before it crested. The wave beat me to the spot and crashed over my head, but I kept my hands on the paddle and shook my head like a dog once I realized I was out of the wave. Miraculously, I had kept enough momentum, and my kayak shot through the wave and deposited me on the other side into open water. The key, as I had learned, to kayak paddling was to extend your hands out in front of your waist and push with one hand/arm while pulling with the opposite.

Our group paddled about 2 miles to another small island beach where we surfed some smaller waves into shore. We all needed a rest for a bit and were excited because the rain had stopped for the moment. It remained cloudy, but the heat was noticeable even through the thick layer of clouds. The warmth felt incredible on my pruned skin, and, of course, no one brought sunscreen on our day's excursion. In two hours of cloudiness, most of us got very sunburned. On the way back to home camp, we had the toughest paddling yet, with a very strong current and wind working against us. It seemed I would paddle and make no progress toward our beach, which looked like a speck in the distance. My travel mates, Jenn and Eileen, wimped out and motioned for Captain Saviche (our supply person who brought things by boat to our beach camp) to tow them in. Meanwhile, with too much pride to give up, both Theresa and I kept going, and I was amazed that the rolling swells were so big that I would actually lose sight of her just 10 feet away as we naturally drifted up and down with each swell. After another very long half hour or more, we made it to the beach and did the usual scramble out and onto the beach, this time with Jimmy's help. High tide was coming in as well, since it was around 2:00 in the afternoon, and the waves reached heights of more than 8–10 feet and crashed in on us and the kayaks. Our adventure was "kicked up" a notch as the waves plunged in closer to our camp and huge logs and debris floated and crashed in with the waves, turning our beach into a white soupy froth. A large group of waves all crashed in and sent our entire group scrambling to keep things from washing out to sea. The kayaks had to be hauled farther up the ridge, and yet another wave ran all the way to the mess tent and to Jeff and Eileen's tent. It swamped the bottoms and soaked everything in its path. This sparked a flurry of shouts and activity to pull all the bags out and stack them as best we could on the mess table. Our tent, because of its location farther back and on a slight hill, escaped any further dampening. Jimmy tried to divert the water around the tents by digging canals, as Theresa had done, but he gave up a short time later and joined us for a group meeting to discuss our options. Alejo had made some calls from his satellite phone and asked for weather updates and possible accommodations if we elected to hike out and around Curu. Soggy and tired, Alejo gave us our options: A, stay one more night in our soaked tents and paddle out at 8 a.m. or, B, hike 2–3 miles through the rain forest and mud right away back to Curu Lodge and then by bus return to San Gildar Hotel before starting the rafting portion of the trip. The majority of our group voted to hike out and try to relax and dry out before setting out again on more wet adventures. Theresa was adamant on not spending one more night in the tent.

So, it was decided after our version of a tribal council that we would load up our packs and Captain Saviche and Jimmy would stay behind and bring all the other supplies later. Alejo, donning a walking stick, led the way along a mucky trail that cut through the forest and opened up a bit into pastures for cattle grazing. As we trudged through mud, we avoided cow pies, and both Theresa and young Jen struggled as their feet kept slipping out of their sandals. They ended up walking through mud and dung alike in bare feet. The rest of us fought off some briars and got nicked up along the way. The trail continued, and we walked up and down steep hills and even scaled a fence. Ironically, it did not rain a drop as we walked back to Curu, but I was drenched nonetheless–in sweat. Our trail eventually led to a more maintained two-track and led us to a grouping of buildings and cottages. While we waited for transportation that would take us back to the ferry, we all huddled on a covered porch as the rain poured down again for a bit.

We waited over an hour while feeling dirty and restless. Some of our group even took showers in the rustic facilities. I opted to wait for a hot hotel shower with real shampoo and soap, so I festered in my stinky, filthy clothes. Finally, a 20-minute "taxi" ride delivered us to the ferry, where most of us promptly fell asleep for the hour ride aboard. Some of our group must have slept too soundly! As we made our way off the boat, we realized that Jeff and Eileen were missing. I watched amused as Jerry, Jeff's dad, had to leap from the walkway as the boat began to pull away. Jeff and Eileen's ill-timed bathroom stop on board led to some anxious moments when we wondered whether we were ever going to make it to our hotel. Luckily, the ferry was docking for the night, so our bus met it at the dock just down the street so we could retrieve our lost companions. We stopped briefly at a Costa Rican fast-food joint for some rice and snacks, and then we bussed back to the city. We rode on a Greyhound-type bus, which gave us plenty of room to stretch out, but our driver kept me awake, as his reckless and fast driving had me a bit worried. As we drove out of the lit area of the small town, we cornered precariously through a patch of dirt road, through the median, and onto a major highway all at a high rate of speed for a bus. I was very excited when, several hours later, we pulled up to the familiar confines of San Gildar. Theresa and I dashed for our room, where I promptly showered and fell into my luxurious bed around 2 a.m.

Tuesday dawned much brighter, and Alejo had told us all to take our time and sleep in, so I took full advantage and kept rolling over and hugging my pillows and blankets while enjoying my half-awake and half-asleep time before actually getting myself up. I called the day in my journal "tourist day" because we did some sightseeing of the less adventurous kind in and around Costa Rica's largest city, San José. The rain delay and early pullout afforded us a day to visit more mainstream attractions, the first being Café Britt, a coffee plantation, restaurant, and gift shop. Café Britt's fun-loving staff led us on a SNL version of a tour while playfully explaining coffee's history, how it is processed, how it is packaged, and, of course, how to properly taste it. Three colorful Costa Ricans walked us to the outskirts of the coffee fields and asked for a volunteer to pick a raw coffee bean, called a "coffee cherry," to demonstrate its color and when it is ready to be harvested. Theresa was the volunteer, but they made it easy for her to select the correct bean. For effect, Café Britt had "planted" a ripe coffee cherry 10 times the normal size on the edge of the field in plain view for all of us. She happily selected the large bean and held it up for our group to see. The tour also included a small production on stage in a small auditorium; we learned of all the different varieties of coffee produced and facts about Costa Rica's ranking relative to the world's producers of coffee. Our last stop was the gift shop, and, like good tourists, we loaded up on many bags of coffee and some necklaces and T-shirts. I bought some Café Britt Light Roast beans to take home. To this day, both Theresa and I import our beans from that very plantation for a smooth, robust cup of coffee—a must for mornings back home.

Next, our group moved on to the Lapaz Waterfall Gardens, where we lunched while overlooking a beautiful hummingbird garden on a ridge high above the rain forest below. Lapaz, as we learned, was owned and operated by an American company, but its features and stunning views were distinctly local. A light rain had followed us on and off that day, but we were able to follow a walkway down to an area to view waterfalls. On the way, we visited a butterfly dome, where I watched the moving larvae of soon-to-be butterflies suspended on the wispy mesh like material that hung on the walls of the dome. We even were treated to a worker, suspended by a cable from the dome's ceiling, who was spraying and attending to the butterflies' every needs. Once out of the dome, I saw Costa Rican plants and foliage up close as we walked through the gardens to where a series of four falls descended into the canyon below. One waterfall crashed down more than 100 feet, and you could stand on a platform and get soaked by the spray if you were so inclined. I had been wet enough the past three days, so I kept my distance. An elaborate series of steps, trails, and staircases connected you to each waterfall viewing area, and the walk back become quite strenuous as I walked up the steep steps. Everywhere, lush greenery and dense foliage dominated the scene, and the gardens themselves were filled with exotic plant species with leaves larger than my head and scores of bright wildflowers lining tiered ledges all the way up to the restaurant at Lapaz. This stunning view from looking up the ridge at the gardens became the subject of a prized photo and later an original watercolor painting. The artist who painted the photo was Julie Hegedus (Theresa's mom), later commissioned by Theresa and given to me as a special holiday gift. It hangs on my wall above my fireplace and reminds me of the natural beauty of that place.

That would mark the end of our tourist day, and we loaded up for a ride back to the city. We did encounter San José gridlock on the way, which gave Alejo an opportunity to point out his wife's stores on the way; they specialized in imported sweaters and clothing. Once back at the hotel, we managed to have dinner at the hotel restaurant and retired somewhat early to the room. An early wake-up call awaited us on Wednesday for a departure to the Caribbean side for whitewater rafting adventures.

The second half of my Costa Rican adventure proved to be wet as well, but not because of rain or tropical depressions. On an early Wednesday morning, we loaded up in our minibus and drove across the country to the Caribbean side (it's only 70 miles from end to end) to Rios Tropicales, the rafting headquarters for our outfitter. En route, we drove through the country's only tunnel, and our excitement grew as the sun began to consistently shine through the clouds. Our group lunched at Rios Tropicales under a covered picnic area laden with wet river gear hanging to dry. After lunch, a short bus ride took us riverside to the mighty Reventezon River for our river orientation from Alejo. I selected a life jacket and a yellow plastic helmet. After further review, I determined this piece of equipment would be of no help to me if I flew out of the raft and hit a rock with my head. Rafting 101 included what to do if thrown from the raft, how to pull someone in the boat from the river, and basic paddle commands such as "paddle forward" or "backpaddle." I mentally logged this info and hoped I would not need to use some of it, particularly the part about falling out and remembering to point your feet down to avoid a rock collision with your upper body or face! Earlier, as we drove down to the river, I had gotten a chance to see it from 800 feet above our put-in. The heavy rains had turned the water a murky brown as it curved through valleys and rockier cliffs farther in the distance. From this vantage point, the river did not seem too menacing, but once we were in the raft, the muddy water seemed to take on a much different personality.

I was excited when we were assigned to a raft, and Theresa and I took our places up front. In our raft behind me were Jenn and her dad, Joe, with Alejo guiding and steering from the backseat. After a brief five minutes of getting comfortable on my perch aside the raft, mild white water grew quickly to churning rapids. We had been warned that the river difficulty in all areas had gone up considerably with the rain and subsequent flooding. The rapids grew in intensity, and we surged ahead and into a "water hole" that tipped the raft sideways and almost vertical to the left. As the raft teetered precariously on its side, I watched my raft mates Theresa and Jen flip backward (much like a scuba diver enters the water) into the churning waves. In a quick and lucky move, I leaned with the boat and avoided the same fate. As the boat fell back onto the surface of the river, Alejo started shouting orders to locate and pull Theresa and Jen back in. The waters settled a bit, and two wet blond heads appeared, and their hands grasped the side of the raft. As I had been instructed, I grabbed Theresa by the shoulders of her life vest and hauled her back in the raft. Theresa was soaked through but did not seem too upset by her dumping and even told me later that she thought Alejo had tipped us on purpose to see how we would react. All back in, the four in our raft learned to paddle in unison and practiced rafting commands, which would become more important as the rapids' difficulty grew. We drifted into an easy section of water, and we all jumped in and floated a bit to cool off. The warm-up of about 1 1/2 hours was a perfect blend of exhilarating paddling through rapids and easy floating and sightseeing. We helped our guides pull the rafts from the water and took off our gear and once again loaded in our bus to drive to Casa Turrire, our happy-hour destination and the night's accommodations. It was one of three small, distinct hotels, this one with 15 rooms and meticulously decorated social areas and patios. We entered the grounds of Casa Turrire through a path lined by perfectly spaced palm trees, and a lake spanned out on both sides, with a volcanic mountain in the distance beyond. My words do no justice to this beautiful place and its tropical charm and warm breezes. The scenery made my happy-hour cocktail one of the best I have ever had. After happy hour and a freshen up, our entire group met for a formal dinner in the Casa's main dining room. Dinner choices included fish, beef, and a pasta selection. Theresa and I both played it safe with the pasta, because we figured we could use the carbs for paddling energy. This turned out to be a wise choice. Theresa distinctly remembers Eileen turning to her and saying, "This beef tastes funny." Well, the next morning, after eating the beef, Eileen was in much distress.

At 8:30 on Thursday, as we convened to head out to our day on the Pacuare River, we learned and "heard" of Eileen's queasy stomach. We milled about in the lobby while hoping she would appear so we could be on our way to the next river adventure. She showed up but was in clear discomfort and stood among us for only a second before dashing into the bathroom adjacent to the lobby. It was impossible not to hear her heaving, and we all felt incredibly bad for her and patiently waited for her to be done retching and board the bus. On this section of the river trip, we had to pack light and cram a few days' worth of clothes in a backpack, as they would be going down the river with us in dry bags in the oar boat with May, another guide. As we headed by bus to our put-in, we stopped at a Costa Rican version of a mini-mart called the Super 2000. I grabbed a beverage and a chocolate bar, and no doubt Eileen got a bottle of stomach-calming liquid.

Also along the route, Alejo had arranged for a visit to a serpentarium, which we all called the snake-a-torium instead. A woman greeted us, and Aljeo translated as she took us into the grounds and a small snake zoo. Minor and his daughter, Nueva, were our guides, both of whom were bona fide snake experts. They described the species, names, and details about any poisonous variety. In glass-covered areas, many types of snakes were housed, including boas, fertile lans, and vipers. To my amazement, Minor donned two metal snake hooks and pulled the wriggly creatures out for us to get a closer view. We were allowed to get about 3 feet from them and snap photos–but no closer. We also made the up-close acquaintance of a famous tree frog and Nueva's pet boa. The boa was wrapped around her neck and arms, and she proudly displayed her pet to us. They also had a dog, but he smartly kept his distance from the boa. We were treated to a tour of their home as well. The home was perched on a steep side hill lined with macadamia trees and coffee fields, and the rain forest stretched out just beyond. The home had clean tile floors, brightly painted walls, and smaller rooms–a simplistic elegance but not extravagant. We said our good-byes and thanked Minor and Nueva for an unforgettable tour, and I also made a small donation to continued snake research. One of the serpentarium's goals was to create antivenin to save people bitten by poisonous snakes.

Back on the bus, Didier, our driver, somehow managed to navigate us down a rutted dirt road and a river that crossed our road. We would have to walk the rest of the steep way down to the river, as the bus had gone as far as it could on this terrain. As we approached the rafts and our launching point, I realized that Jimmy and Randall had prepared lunch and displayed it for us on an overturned raft. Our two young and handsome guides had sliced up pineapple, watermelon, mangos, and also meats and cheeses to make sandwiches. I took in the view of our two guides in their board shorts and then munched happily on the ripe fruit and put together a tasty sandwich before putting on my required gear.

Theresa and I must have proved our mettle the previous day, as Alejo asked us to take positions up front again. Sweet! The Pacuare was narrower and more technical than the Reventezon, and the rapids came in quicker intervals. The rapids were classified as Class III and IV rapids. About halfway down our day's float, we pulled rafts ashore and climbed up a waterfall trail to a pool created by a small 20-foot waterfall. We all swam in the natural pool, and the brave ones, which included Theresa, climbed up the 20-foot wall of rock and plunged down into the bubbling waters below. I selected to stay down and play in the waterfall spray as my daredevil companion showed me up. After our side adventure, we had more paddling to attend to on some rough sections of the Pacuare. The white water and waves really started to crash with authority into and over the boat. Many times, as I reached forward to paddle, I was completely immersed in a wall of water and dug my toes into my foothold as best I could. It was so exciting and scary all at the same time, and my adrenaline flowed as I paddled, with Alejo's voice sounding in my ear. Right before beaching the raft at our camp for the day, we had to maneuver a difficult section, and the other rafters in our group watched us as we attempted to navigate through the rapids to safety. We ploughed ahead, and I could not help but let out a yell after each wave hit me. I would quickly shake my head from side to side to clear my wet hair and the water from my eyes. Alejo barked out two last "paddle hards," and we made it safely to the other side of the river and calmer waters near our camp. No one fell out that day, so we all felt quite good about our performance.

The Pacuare River Camp consisted of a large main building on stilts, with a thatched leafy roof, and two- and three-story bungalows situated on the steep side hill above, which were to be our sleeping quarters. The huts and main building looked to be constructed from the resources in the rain forest that dominated the landscape, such as bamboo, palm leaves, etc. The rustic buildings seemed very charming, and I was even surprised to learn that two other tiny structures housed men's and women's toilets, running water, and even showers. After hauling the raft ashore, our entire group walked up a hill and then across a series of narrow bridges to a three-story bungalow, where we all chose a room. The bridges and my bungalow overlooked the river and some steep rocky crevasses that lined the outer boundaries of the river canyon. I took off my wet gear and laid it out over a nearby railing to dry, but I had learned to get used to a damp dry because of the heat and humidity. I leaned on the railing and took in the view and noted the constant roar of the rapids in my ears. I learned that the entire camp was powered by the water rushing down the steep hill through a system that fueled turbines. So far, my river experiences had been very exciting, and the river camp accommodations were unique and comfortable. Over the din of the river, I heard Alejo's voice calling us down for happy hour, served promptly at 5 p.m. That day, we were treated to authentic piña coladas, and while we sipped our drinks, four of us played a competitive game of Uno as dinner was being prepped. We battled the bugs a bit as evening came, but dinner was once again delicious, featuring home-cooked local dishes. We were served pork chops with a homemade pineapple sauce and a side of white rice. I also relished a cold cerveza, an Imperial, with my meal. We thanked our cooks, Alejo, Randal, and Jimmy, and made them pose with us in their aprons for a photo. I set off shortly after to do some reading and relax in my bungalow. My night faded into sleep as I heard bugs bouncing off my screened window, and the river's constant rush lulled me into relaxation.

The next day, Friday, we took off from rafting and elected to go on an "optional bird-watching hike," as was the title in the original itinerary. In actuality, the hike turned into exploring several waterfalls and hiking up and down very steep muddy slopes filled with dense vegetation. Both Theresa and I had Kilimanjaro flashbacks as we panted and the sweat dripped profusely off the tips of our noses while we leaned up the hill on this hike. I don't recall sweating like that ever before; your entire body beaded up like water on a freshly waxed car. Up and up we went, and we discarded our shoes in a gorge that housed a beautiful waterfall surrounded by dense tropical vegetation. The gorge was lined with large rocks and boulders, and they formed natural pools for us to swim in. Most of our group found a good spot to lounge around to lie partially in the water and soak in the late-morning sun. We also received a special treat from Alejo: he gave each of us a rainforest foot massage with clay that he made on the spot by rubbing smooth small stones on a nearby boulder mixed with some water to create a creamy substance that he smoothed on the bottoms of our feet. Soooo nice! After, I had lain in the shallow part of the river and closed my eyes for a quick siesta but wound up watching my travel mates slide on their bottoms down a section of smooth rocks into a pool of water below. Eventually, we moved on and started to make our way carefully back down, sometimes with the assistance of Randal and Jimmy. Then we started back up again a steeper and narrower trail, and Jimmy had to hack some branches with his machete to clear a path through the dense greenery. After a half hour of trekking, I saw my shoes were caked with mud, but by that point, we had arrived at the base of a 50-foot waterfall, where I took my turn and let the water pummel my head and shoulders. It was a very powerful rush of water, and I could not stand upright in the natural downward force. It was exhilarating to duck under for a second and then step back out into the waterfall spray. I had not showered in two days, so the powerful water no doubt cleaned off a layer of grime and perhaps exfoliated a layer of skin off my face and shoulders. Still dripping, we set off back to camp, and, feeling a bit tired, I found a hammock and set about reading a book for a while. After a bout of restlessness, I walked down the riverbank area and found a large boulder to lean on and watched a small waterfall cascade down into the main river. The sun gave way to clouds, and at about 4:00 in the afternoon, thunder and lightning split the air, so I came in to avoid being soaked. I sat under the open-air mess hall structure and was treated to a glass of "jungle juice" (I think spiked with Costa Rican rum), garnished with pineapple and watermelon. I may have had one too many, as I felt a bit queasy later that evening and retired early to my room. I fell asleep but woke up many times to wipe the perspiration from my face, and I would lay and listen to sounds above me from the other bungalows until I drifted off into a steamy sleep.

The next day was truly an adventure as we plunged down the river canyon through rain-swollen white water. At 8 a.m. Alejo made the announcement that it was safe to make the run of 18 miles downriver. The rain and flooding had threatened to cancel our rafting, but luckily we hit a day of optimal conditions. That day was by far the most fun and challenging day on the water. Once again, my oar mate Theresa and I were chosen for the front, no doubt for our consistent and strong paddling efforts from before! I paddled much harder right away and more frequently, as the rapids' intensity had gone up. In a short few minutes, we pulled rafts up on some rocks and clambered up on huge boulders to get a look at the first run of technical white water. Alejo pointed out our route to the right of a large rock formation in the middle of the river, and we watched as Randall ventured down in his kayak (but on the left). Alejo explained how we would navigate all the way to the right side and have to duck under some tree branches and then begin paddling hard to avoid being pulled into a large water hole. We all hopped back into the raft with anticipation and were treated immediately to Alejo barking orders to paddle. We forced the raft to the right with a few strokes, and my helmet smacked against the low-lining branches. After passing through the branches, I looked up just in time to see the river engulf the raft and turn us backward in a huge hole as giant waves pounded all sides. Alejo yelled at all of us to lean in, and simultaneously I was hit head-on by a wave of water that knocked me and Theresa into the middle of the raft. With Alejo's pleas, we all regained our composure and began to try to paddle. He helped us to turn the raft, and, with much effort, we snuck out of the churning white water and continued through many other rapids with names such as Dos Montanas, the Lower and Upper Huachas, and many others I can't name now. The rapids came in very quick sequences, with little time to recover. It was such a rush in the front of the raft as we encountered each new surge and I reached into muddy white water with my paddle. My arms were beginning to tire as we made it through a long stretch of rapids. We looked back to see how our other raft was doing and realized the supply boat had flipped over and was stuck in the churning rapids behind us. Luckily, May, who had been oaring the boat, had swum under the raft and floated up ahead toward us. We were glad he was all right, but we all watched helplessly as our supplies were stuck in a "washing machine." It finally broke free and started down toward us. Alejo shocked us all into action to help retrieve the boat and sent us scrambling into positions to grab paddles in our raft. As I stepped back in the raft, I slipped and fell into Theresa, who laughed at my fall before starting to paddle. Once that crisis was over, the water calmed to a slow gurgle, so we jumped into the river to float a bit through a short-lived calm section in a narrow gorge. We spotted the supply boat up ahead, so Alejo motioned for me to swim back to the raft. He grabbed me by the shoulders and life vest and pulled me in; he must not have realized his strength as I shot into the boat and landed in a pile of paddles at the feet of Joe and Jen. We laughed again as I took my spot up front and we floated down to the overturned raft. We all got out and as a team turned the boat over and checked to make sure all the gear was still intact. The dry bags housed all of our clothes and backpacks, so we worried a bit about how wet they might be. We chatted with those on the other raft and learned that they had lost paddlers several times; on one occasion we pulled in Jeff and then transferred him back to the other boat. No one fell out that day in our raft, but Jimmy's crew had not been as fortunate. The sun warmed our backs as we talked about our day on the river and paddled toward our take-out for lunch and showers. We all helped pull the rafts ashore and loaded them on a trailer and started to dry things out. I popped a pill at lunch to calm my queasy stomach, and we had to say our good-byes to Randal, May, and Jimmy. Back on the bus, we headed to San José, and I lamented over my soggy journal with ink running on each page, thus blurring my daily entries. I laid it on the seat to dry and hoped I could decipher it later. We would head back and get cleaned up for a final farewell dinner with our group. On the bus, we chatted about the rapids and laughed at our cuts, bruises, and bug bites. The three days of rain were forgotten because the last four were beautiful sunny days with evening showers to accompany each happy hour. We did learn that the coast where we had stayed was hit by a tropical depression; 16-foot waves flooded coastline areas and then moved toward Nicaragua, where the storm delivered more damage. Our guides told us that had not happened in more than six years and how unlucky it was that we were camping near the shoreline where it had hit. Looking back, I realize how much more adventurous those three days had become. Though the rain dampened things a bit and kept us from snorkeling and lounging in the sun, it really took the adventure level up a notch and had made for quite a good story to tell.

Later that night, we joined our group at an open-air café and snapped some group photos and exchanged e-mails so we could share pictures later. The restaurant was called Quibolo, and we enjoyed yet another excellent meal while thanking Alejo for leading us on such an exciting trip. Alejo gave both Theresa and me a bear hug and thanked us both for being such good paddlers. Of course, I smiled and beamed inside: I liked being an A student!

As I walked back to our hotel for the last night to prepare for an early-morning departure and a full day of travel, I realized that I had to go to work on Monday. I quickly pushed that thought aside and smiled as I remembered my nine days of white sand beaches, rain forests, the warmth of the tropical sun, and the incredible people of Costa Rica. "Costa Rica" means "rich coast," and my contention is that it is aptly and perfectly named.

Photos from top to bottom/left to right: Laura with Theresa posing with the Lapaz Waterfall Gardens as a backdrop; Rafting on Class IV, V's on the Reventezon River swollen after a tropical depression; A poor woman's umbrella; My group of 7 on the Costa Rica trip; Laura jumps from the rock into a "safe" section of river for a quick cool off.

CHAPTER 5

Vegas! What's the Big Whoop?
Las Vegas, USA–October 25–29, 2002

Well, Vegas was the first trip I had ever been on that was FREE–but judging by how little I wrote in my journal on this particular vacation, I am very glad it was free. With a mere $10 raffle ticket, purchased at a local charity auction that spring, I had won a flight and weekend stay in Vegas, complete with accommodations at the Bellagio! It was very shocking to hear my name called as the winner, especially after I had announced to my entire table, "I am not much of a gambler, so I don't really need to go to Vegas." Their reaction and mine were a combination of laughter and surprise as the announcer pulled the winning ticket and yelled, "Laura Holmes is the winner!" Since I had been invited to this charity event by my good friend Theresa and her family, it seemed only fitting that she should be the one to accompany me. The prize was a trip for two, and I really did not want to go alone to Vegas.

We took a late flight out to Vegas from Detroit Metro and did not arrive at the glitz and neon until after 8 p.m. local time. It felt like 11 p.m. to me, Eastern time, and the Spartan flight had Theresa and I both famished. As we cabbed over to the Bellagio, we agreed to check in quickly and find something to eat right away. The famous Strip was a blur of blinking lights, and it was difficult to take in, as each casino blended into the next. Our cabbie deposited us at the revolving doors of our hotel, and as I entered, I was amazed at the level of noise and the constant whir of gamblers on all types of slots, roulette wheels, and craps or dice tables. It was loud, but I tried to focus on what everyone had said to me before leaving. Leading up to the trip, each time I mentioned the Bellagio, each person went absolutely gaga over that name, and they assured me that it was the most glamorous place to stay in Vegas. Since this had occurred no less than five times before leaving, it had made quite an impression on me, so I was led to believe I would be staying at resort nirvana with every luxury one could imagine. Check-in was uneventful in the impressive lobby with our crisp-looking clerk; he suggested a room with a view of the signature musical fountains gracing the resort's entrance. We set off to the eighth floor to stow our luggage. I keyed in and was immediately hit by a wave of stale cigarette smoke partially masked by cleaning products. Both Theresa and I turned on our heels and went straight away to the front desk to get another nonsmoking room. Minutes later, we finally arrived at room 10-49 with a less than spectacular view of the resort's backside and parking lot, but it certainly smelled much better. I quickly freshened up, as Theresa was bonking on lack of nourishment. We left our room behind in search of food and drink. I selected a place back on the main floor called Noodles, a nifty little Asian spot that would fill our bellies with carbs. Of course, in Vegas, just people watching in the restaurant kept me entertained until my bowl of noodles arrived. I absolutely pounded down my food and washed it down with a beer, which gave me a buzz–unless that was just the din of the casino. I realized Vegas had a way of making you feel like you should try to "go until you drop," with all the excitement and lures of the casino. For me, it proved to be the roulette wheel on the first night. Theresa was looking pretty tired, but she hung in long enough for me to win $80 and then lose it all again. I had started with a crisp $20 changed into $5 chips and was pleased to enjoy a free drink on the house while I gambled. But, as it usually goes in Vegas, you go up, and then you come back down. Empty-handed at my first gambling attempt, I headed up to the room and quickly collapsed into a pile of down pillows on a precisely made bed. I peered at my digital clock on the bedside table, and it read 2 a.m. I closed my eyes and realized it was 5 a.m. Michigan time.

My eyes opened pretty early to some brightness coming through the window, and I realized where I was and started to get excited about doing some exploring. I showered and found some comfortable clothes and shoes for walking around and then very abruptly realized I was starving. Theresa and I headed down again to the main floor to find a breakfast place, but every restaurant or buffet had a huge line, so we opted to go outside and across the street in search of the elusive egg and a cup of coffee. Not many diners but plenty of strip clubs and casinos, so we finally settled for McDonald's and savored an Egg McMuffin washed down with coffee and juice. Next, we made our way inside the Aladdin Resort and into the Desert Passage Shops that wound through many corridors. Small boutique-style shops lined the hallways and carried overpriced and pretentious clothes, hats, accessories, and a variety of eclectic collectibles. I meandered aimlessly, not really in the mood to shop, and after we spent an hour walking the desert-themed Aladdin, the passageway gave way to the Paris Casino and Resort, complete with a pretty impressive replica of the Eiffel Tower dominating the entrance. I made my way through the main casino and waved to Theresa to follow me to a bar flanking the edge of the casino area. I noticed that football games were on at the bar, so I ordered a Bloody Mary, spicy with extra olives, and sat down for a bit. Ironically, as I looked up from my Bloody Mary, I noticed that the woman I had sat next to on the plane ride on the way to Vegas was standing at the bar with her husband. "What are the odds," I thought to myself, "that I would run into Jill from the airplane ride?" I laughed to myself because I was in the capital of "people attempting to beat the odds." I said hello to Jill, who happily introduced me to her husband, Casey. She was equally surprised to see me again. After a brief chat and a well wish for fun in Vegas, Theresa and I set off again on foot to see some more of the Strip. By day, Vegas was not quite as impressive without the barrage of dazzling and moving lights, but it was still overwhelming in magnitude, which led to us ambling around without purpose, just gawking at each casino's grand and themed entrances. After a couple miles of walking, we made it back to the room to relax for a bit but encountered our maid changing our sheets, so we hung out and waited for her departure before throwing ourselves on the beds to stretch. We had an hour to rest before getting ready for an evening out Vegas style. The night would feature an overpriced dinner at a French restaurant, Le Cirque; tickets to Cirque de Soleil's O; and a nightcap hovering over a Bellagio roulette table. To make it to the show on time, we dined early-bird-style at 5:30 but enjoyed an excellent bottle of French red served by a delightfully handsome waiter. The food proved to be equally as delightful as the waiter, and the crème brûlée dessert was a fitting end to our five-course dinner. With very full bellies, we made our way back through the casino to the theater that housed Cirque's set for O still inside the Bellagio. I settled into my third-row seat and marveled at the moving and ever-transitioning stage seemingly made of water, complete with a cast of actors and acrobats that left me spellbound. The performance was truly a visual feast and my favorite memory on this trip. The acrobatic stunts and the strength and flexibility of the performers really captivated my attention, and I was impressed by the way many emotions found their way in to the performance: sometimes serious precision, sometimes humor, and sometimes passion. I paid $129 for that ticket, but I really felt as if I will never see anything on stage quite like that again. I am not sure how long the performance lasted, but I reluctantly left my seat at the end and walked back out into the loud casino. My nightcap was a cocktail at the roulette table. I started with $20 in chips and played a while, betting conservatively on black/red or odd/even instead of single numbers. As you can tell, I am not a high roller. I also placed my chips on the sequences of numbers to increase my odds and stayed away from choosing single numbers. I would watch each time in anticipation as the marble would bounce around the wheel and finally settle on a lucky digit. I did pretty well and managed to make $100 from my $20, so I thought it best to go to bed a winner. I walked to a counter and cashed in my chips and found Theresa, who was equally ready to call it a night.

The next morning was much like Groundhog Day, as I went downstairs in search of breakfast only to learn in line that the buffet would run us each $47. I am not a cheap person, but it seemed absolutely preposterous that I would spend almost $50 on a spoonful of eggs, a piece of toast, and coffee. Theresa and I exchanged glances as the hostess eyed us impatiently, and then we both turned on our heels and got out of line and left the Bellagio breakfast buffet. For the second time, we entered the Aladdin Casino, and inside we found a restaurant called the Zanzabar Café, where we happily settled in. To celebrate, we asked for a round of mimosas and placed orders for hearty breakfast plates that included eggs, hash browns, greasy sausage patties, and toast. We chatted over coffee, sipped mimosas, and discussed what we would do that day in Vegas. Since it was Sunday, we planned to find the ESPN Zone in New York, New York, and watch the pitiful Lions play. I finished up my breakfast, and the busy wait staff cleared our table and our waitress dropped off our bill and wished us a wonderful day. I casually picked it up to take a look at what we owed, and as I scanned to the bottom, I started to laugh out loud as I read the total to Theresa. "Our breakfast bill is $47," I pronounced in a fit of laughter and handed it to a disbelieving Theresa. She was equally as amazed that everywhere you went, breakfast always seemed to be 50 bucks.

Moving on, we walked off our breakfast and then some. We entered New York's resort, dominated by replicas of the city's famous skyscrapers and a rollercoaster meandering through the maze of buildings and structures. Inside, the line was very long to get a seat in the Zone, with all the NFL games going on, so we gave up that idea and searched for another place we might catch the game. We were in luck: as we walked closer to the casino, a large room had been converted into a sports theater, with three huge big-screen TVs all showing live football games and offering free seating. We did watch the Lions for a

bit, and they did lose as we expected! Then we set off on foot again.
My other stops that day included the Excalibur and then, across the
Strip, the MGM, where we got hopelessly lost in the winding corridors
and shops. We continued on and later that afternoon encountered
Caesar's Palace and, finally, the Venetian, which was my favorite resort.
My feet were really starting to get sore by that point, so I remember just
sitting and watching a street actor dressed in white robes who would
hold perfectly still to the amusement of people who would step within
inches of the character's face or arms. The Venetian was equipped with
actual water canals and longboat rides made famous in Venice. The
Italian flare was evident everywhere, and to fit in, Theresa and I found
an Italian restaurant for happy hour and some dinner.

We walked all the way back to the Bellagio in the dark and
watched as night descended on Vegas and the buzz of gambling and
partying took hold of the scene. I remember a bit more gambling later
that evening, but my journal lacked some serious detail at that point
and basically trailed off into nothing. I don't think I even bothered to
record our last day or the return trip. So, I end this chapter abruptly,
as did my journal, with a mental note that I prefer a different brand of
vacations: ones with mountains to hike or rivers to raft, for example.
Vegas is a marvel of architecture and amazing recreations, but I prefer
the real versions of the Eiffel Tower and New York skyscrapers. My
thought is that a trip to Vegas should be about a three-night max and
you are covered.

CHAPTER 6

Mooossseee!
Alaska, USA–May 31–June 8, 2003

I would argue that Alaska ranks for many as a favorite travel destination and a must-see for any adventure traveler. I found myself lucky enough to visit the great state in the summer of 2003. This trip materialized when my travel buddy, Theresa, whom I had visited Africa and Costa Rica with previously, informed me that her high school classmate and good friend, Susan Wolski-Stokes, now lived in Anchorage. Sue had invited Theresa to make a visit and had offered up her home as a starting point for some Alaskan sightseeing, hiking, and biking. Sue, her husband, Earl, and two boys had moved to Anchorage in 2001 for a job opportunity, and they had gladly settled in and took full advantage of all the area's outdoor activities and natural resources. So, by association, I was lucky enough to be invited to join in on an Alaskan adventure. I gladly accepted the invitation and hoped I could keep up with Sue's friends, who were already planning some epic group bike and hiking trips during our visit.

The front end of this trip featured a full day of travel. The summary of our route to Anchorage included leaving Grand Rapids for Detroit and, five hours later, arriving in Seattle for a three-hour layover, before ultimately continuing on to Anchorage, where we would be arriving at 11:30 p.m. local time. Flying into Anchorage was a unique sight from the air, dominated equally by white-capped mountains and huge inlets of crisp blue water. Even travel weary, I was anxious to be on the ground to see Anchorage and the views across the famous Cook Inlet. Once we landed and after collecting our gear, we proceeded to the rental car counter. We ended up renting a rather beat-up Honda

Accord–you could tell by the car's rap sheet the rental agent handed us, with many notes about dings, scratches, and a large chip in the front window. But, Theresa turned the key and it started, so we headed off to find Sue and Earl's place on the outskirts of the city. We exited on Rabbit Run Drive and continued up a slope, where we turned onto smaller and smaller dirt roads. Finally, the road ended and opened to a handsome two-story log cabin, nestled in pines and hardwoods, with a view out over the inlet. Though it was midnight, it actually appeared dusklike at this time of night, as Alaskan summers featured more than 20 hours of daylight per day. It was nice to be able to see the gorgeous surroundings, and I was even more excited by the accommodations at the late hour, which looked much more impressive and cozy than a cheap hotel chain. Though it was very late, Sue greeted Theresa and me at the door and gave us welcoming hugs as we lugged in our bags and backpacks. After bringing in most of our stuff from the Accord, we sat upstairs in the living room and shared a glass of red wine with Sue and chatted briefly about what she had in store for our week. I started yawning hopelessly around 1 a.m., so Sue showed us both to our rooms down on the main level. My room turned out to be next to her sons' room (Witt and Beck). Theresa's room was just down the hall past the sauna room. I fell into an exhausted sleep after throwing on pajama pants and a tank top and slipping under the covers.

Still trying to adjust to the four-hour time change, I was actually up early on the first morning, and by 8 a.m. we were in the car with Sue at the wheel, driving toward Aleyeska Ski Resort for breakfast and some warm-up sightseeing. It was a 40-minute trip south on the Seward Highway, and I sat in the backseat and admittedly gawked at the scenery like a tourist! The huge bay called Cook Inlet was to my right, with the mud flats leading up to the banks, and a range of 4,000-foot mountains lay behind us and across the inlet. It was truly unspoiled beauty, and my words cannot capture the vast space and the blueness of the water and sky, along with the new green of the soon-to-be summer.

During our drive, three bald eagles flew near and over the car, and I could actually see their talons stretched and open as they swooped down to the water, no doubt searching for breakfast as well. At one of many scenic pull-offs, I snapped some panoramic shots of the bay, and we also watched some native Alaskans dip-netting for hooligan in a river feeding into the bay. I was amazed as they netted four or five fish each time they swooshed the net through the water. No fishing pole or bait needed in Alaska! A few miles later, we pulled into the base of Aleyeska Ski Resort, where a quaint restaurant served the three of us a plate of eggs with spinach and mushrooms. It was delicious, and I put away two cups of coffee while still working on the time acclamation. After breakfast, we bought tram tickets for a train that would transport us to the top of the ski hill and a viewing area next to the restaurant that was now closed after ski season. The ride up was amazing as the view became even more spectacular than that from the car ride earlier. Once out of the tram, we were greeted by a brisk wind, and I slipped on a ski hat to keep my sensitive ears warm. We all walked to the deck area and looked out over one of the most amazing views I have ever seen. No hiking was allowed on the ski hill, so after some photo ops, we rode back down. Our second stop was the Portage Lake and Byron Glacier Area and Visitors Center. The weather had quickly turned from our blue sky start to windy, rainy, and very chilly. Because of the conditions, we opted to head inside and check out the visitors center, where I learned information about glacier movement and the area's wildlife. Even ice worms had an exhibit of their own. Another exhibit that we checked out was a detailed description of how rescues were performed on the mud flats of Cook Inlet. The mud flats looked like an inviting shore and beach but could be treacherous because of the silt and the ebb and flow of the tide. Many people had walked out onto the mud flats and sunk into the silty sand, and they got stuck as the tide came in. I made a mental note to stay clear of the flats on this trip. We ventured back outside to check out the Portage Glacier, which was sandwiched in a mountain pass, making the ice appear a crisp blue color. Large chunks of the glacier had broken off and settled in Portage Lake; many odd shapes jutted up from the water and close to the parking area, where I was able to take some photos of the glacier and the surrounding lake. The rain really started coming down, so it forced us back in the car, and we headed back to home base for some lunch.

Back at Sue's, I lunched with Witt and Beck, and as they munched, they peeked at me with shy smiles. After lunch, to cement my newfound friendship, I played pitch and catch with them with a football in the driveway, and they both scurried around and scooped up the ball and fired it back to me. The boys were pretty jacked up after playtime and because they knew we were going to ride bikes at Kincaid Park that afternoon. We changed into biking gear and loaded up the Suburban nicknamed "Arnold" and racked the bikes on the back. Kincaid Park was just off the outskirts of Anchorage, with both paved and a variety of single-track trails to choose from for biking adventures. That day, we chose the easy paved route as both Sue and Earle pulled the boys in carriers behind and Theresa and I got used to our borrowed mountain bikes. We set off on a leisurely pace, and we encountered and watched several moose grazing just off the trail. Besides the moose, the views of the city set against the inlet and the mountain range beyond were captivating. On our ride back around the loop, we pedaled, with Theresa in the lead and me next and then Sue and Earle pulling the boys. I kept Theresa in my sight, and on a slight downhill with a curve at the end, I watched as Theresa zipped around that corner, just a second after a young male moose stepped onto the path and blocked my passage. I rode my brakes to a stop and motioned for everyone behind me to stop and look ahead. The moose stood half on and half off the trail as he munched on something in the foliage. We waited patiently for him to clear the path before continuing on, while a traffic jam of sorts built up behind me as bikers all took in our dilemma and watched the unfazed moose eat lunch. Finally, an exasperated and impatient male biker walked up past me and started to yell and make motions, which did get the moose's attention. The animal then ambled off the trail so we could pass. Theresa was considerably ahead of us by that time, as she had just missed the roadblock, so we caught up to her and filled her in on her near miss. After the biking adventure and our first moose encounter, our day was completed with a trip to Mooses Tooth for pizza and microbrews. Later, back at home base, after a sauna and hot shower, I made it to only 10ish.

The Road to Denali

Theresa and I had planned to spend Monday and Tuesday exploring the Denali National Park area. So, the next morning after bagels, coffee, and good-bye kisses from the boys, we set off by 9 a.m. toward one of the nation's most famous national parks, home to Mount McKinley. A stop at Carr's Grocery landed us a cheap cooler, focaccia bread sandwiches, and other snacks for our ride. With 300 miles to travel, we first drove through Anchorage and then across the river flats into Palmer. Then we continued north on Glenn Highway and opted for the road less traveled and turned toward Hatcher Pass and the Independence Mine area. Along this route, I was startled out of my driving daze when a moose darted across the road in front of us, narrowly missing our front bumper! "MOOOOOSSSSSSEEEEEEE!" I yelled at the top of my lungs, startling Theresa out of her daze as well. Much more alert now, I followed a rocky riverbed to my right along the roadside, only to eventually come to a "road closed" barrier that blocked any further progress up that road. The pass was obviously still closed because of snow and ice, so we had to backtrack south to Wasilla and then up Highway 5 toward Denali. The dominant Alaskan range was visible now on our left, north of Wasilla, and the views became even more spectacular as each mile passed. Denali Park also marked our first view of McKinley from afar, so we stopped at several pull-offs for pictures. About 30–40 miles south of the park entrance, we also caught glimpses of the Alaskan railroad winding its way near the road and on the banks of the Nanana River. We played a game of chase with the snaking train and sped up ahead of it to gain a vantage point to catch a photo as it passed near the highway we traveled. I noted that the passengers from the tour and passenger cars waved at us while we captured their digital images. The train was a good distraction from the long drive, and shortly after, around 3 p.m., we arrived at our accommodations for the night. We had rented a rustic cabin for just one night near the park entrance, where we stowed our bags and excitedly continued on to the visitor center to get details on hiking trails and secure our shuttle bus tickets, which I had ordered online weeks earlier. With that done, Theresa was starving, so we found Alpen Glow Restaurant on a bluff overlooking the river and ordered lunch. I enjoyed my $10 hamburger and decided not to complain because of the awesome view. It sure beat the $50 breakfast I had in Vegas. The range of mountains extended farther than you could see, all with snow-capped peaks looking cold and ominous. Fully nourished, we set off to conquer the Mount Healy trail. We donned day packs and water bottles, and on the first half mile, our only challenge on this flat section was a flooded bridge, which we navigated by balancing on the handrailssee photo. The next quarter-mile brought us to some rustic benches and an excellent panoramic vista. The remainder of the hike was pretty steep, and we slowed our pace as we switched backed over the rocky face. The vegetation was a combination of willows and spruce, and then higher up, it gave way to rocky shale and scree. The elevation gain to 3,500 feet made it moderately strenuous, and we panted on the final uphill section, but it felt good to hike after being in the car much of the day. At the trail end and top of Healy, we were greeted with excellent views again but also a few raindrops, so we cut our gawking short and headed back down. With a hike under our belt and still battling the four-hour time change, we headed back to Denali Cabins for the night. Theresa encountered a barely lukewarm shower, so I opted for the hot tub for a few minutes instead. I lounged in the hot water, closed my eyes, and enjoyed the relaxing water over tired and sore muscles. Lights were out by 11 p.m., though the sky was not completely dark in Alaska's famous midnight sun.

My Tuesday morning got rolling around 8 a.m. with some coffee and rubbery eggs, but that did not damper the excitement to get into the park on the 9:30 shuttle bus. Theresa and I and about 30 others piled in to a converted school bus, which served as the park's internal shuttle, since no cars were allowed past certain checkpoints in the park. We had planned to get off the bus and do some day hiking and then reconnect with the shuttle later in the day. In the back of the bus, I took a seat and listened as Chuck, our driver, gave us the inside scoop on the park's sights. He directed the bus over a bumpy dirt road, and we quickly had our first game spotting of several distant caribou. Next, a bus mate pointed out some Dall sheep high above us in the rock overhangs and perched on the steep side hills. I did not mind the bumpy ride, especially when treated to scenery of that caliber. The bus made stops at Teklanika River, Polychrome Overlook, and then Toklat River, which is where Theresa and I made our departure to hike a bit on our own. Near the river, we ate a lunch consisting of a sandwich and some potato chips, and we took stock of our surroundings and decided which way we would head on our adventure. After slinging on my day pack, I crossed through a pretty wide stony river bed and then crossed several smallish streams that gave way to a mossy bank that started us up a ridge. Theresa had spotted a pack of Dall sheep on that ridge, so we took about 15 minutes and clambered up to within zoom lens distance of several sheep. I am sure the sheep were amused by our stalking technique as we tried to subtly approach so we could capture their image. I distinctly remember the introductory talk from Chuck on the bus and how important it was NOT to approach any wildlife, but we decided that the ridge the sheep grazed upon just so happened to be the best ridge to hike up as well. We were rewarded with some good photos of the Dall that showed their impressive racks and thick white woolylike coats. We returned to our route up the ridge and made our way back down, of course taking in the far-off vista of McKinley some 50 miles away, flanked by what seemed a never-ending expanse of mountains. Once back down the ridge and navigating through the river crossings, we began walking near the park road and flagged the first bus heading farther into the park to the Eilson Center. We showed our park pass to Mona, the driver of the bus, who we learned was a Michigan native who now lived permanently in the Denali area. She seemed happy to transport a couple of Michiganders down the road. Then we all were excited to spot a mother grizzly bear and her rare triplet cubs up on a ridge to the north of us! After just two more miles, Eilson Center was the end of the line for vehicle transport, so we said good-byes to Mona and followed a worn footpath up to the Eilson vista, where we hoped to catch better views of the misty and often shrouded McKinley peak. With tired legs, we meandered back down and walked around inside the Eilson Center and read about the park's history, wildlife, and McKinley mountaineering lore. That helped pass the time until the 3:45 bus that would take us back to the park entrance. The ride back was long but awesome, as it provided the vantage point to close-ups of the momma bear and her cubs again, this time much nearersee photo. The grizzly, with her cubs close by, dug for vine roots and was quite focused on her task as the cubs playfully walked around near her and often stood on their hind legs to check out their surroundings. I was glued to this sight and leaned as far as I could out my small window to watch the bears. Everyone on the bus was silent at the driver's request as we all watched mesmerized and snapped photos. After some time, we continued to Polychrome, and we were again rewarded with views of Dall sheep just 40 feet away from the bus. As a bonus, a caribou and moose crossed the road right alongside the vehicle a bit farther up. It took three hours to return because top speed was, at best, 30 mph, with the frequent stops for game viewing. No one complained. Once back to our car, we chatted about how awesome it was to have seen the bears so close, and we readied ourselves for the long ride back. We grabbed espresso drinks and fueled up the car, pointing it south. The ride back featured the best views of McKinley yet, as the sun shone brightly and the clouds had disappeared from earlier. Within a 45-mile stretch, we stopped no less than eight times to get photos of the incredible peak and the surrounding range. I just could not stop gawking. On our drive later that evening, the sun finally started to set around 11 p.m., about the time we made it into the outskirts of Anchorage. As I watched the scenery fly by, I realized that a day and a half was not enough time to give Denali its due–especially a park with more than six million acres, bigger than the state of Massachusetts. At least we gave it a shot.

There wasn't too much relaxing and lying around at Sue's, as she had cooked up some plans for our Wednesday. I did sleep in a bit, but over breakfast, she covered the day's itinerary. First, she told us, "We'll head into town and pick up Theresa's rental bike, and then you two can climb Flattop Mountain for a warm-up, and then we'll go biking later with my group of friends at Kincaid." It sounded like the Eco-Challenge to me and Theresa, and I exchanged worried glances with her about making it through the day unscathed. To start our adventure, we loaded up "Arnold" again with Sue and the boys, and we hit the bike shop and also REI, where we found the latest outdoorsy camping necessities. Theresa bought new hiking shoes and a hat, and I scored a new pair of black shorts. For lunch, we enjoyed some Alaskan sunshine on Sue's deck and a lunch of mac and cheese. Early that afternoon, with directions from Sue to the trailhead, we drove a short distance to nearby Flattop Mountain, a popular day hike in the area. The sun shone, so we hiked in shorts but in long sleeves, with the gusty wind. The first part of the trail was quite easy, called Blueberry Loop, and as you glanced back, you could get a view of Anchorage set against the blue of the bay. We did not glance too long, since Sue had us on a tight time schedule for the day and we had to be back in time to go biking later. The wide trail turned quickly from hard pack to loose rocks and a series of switchbacks. We continued up and made our way around the saddle to the final 200 feet, where the wind pick up considerably, cooling me quickly, with the perspiration on my skin. Carefully now, Theresa and I picked our route for solid toeholds and scrambled up rocks and boulders in places. The last 30 feet was quite steep, but it opened to a flat plateau (thus the name) at 3,500 feet in elevation. I added a stone to the pile of summit rocks and then took in the panoramic view for several minutes. The wind was brisk, so it forced me to head down quickly. Coming down was precarious and slippery, as snow still lined some of the crevices and shaded areas, so I stepped, slid, and scrambled down the steep sections and tried to be patient until I found proper footing. The sections of snow and rock gave way to a steady downhill plod, which emphasized a dull ache in my quads. The downhills seemed much tougher on my leg muscles, and I noticed a tightening for the next 30 minutes. Making our way back down to the trailhead, we checked our watches and saw we had made the round trip in 2 1/2 hours. We both agreed that Sue would be happy with that time and headed back for phase II of the Wednesday challenge.

At 6 p.m. our multisport day continued, and I changed from hiking shorts into biking shorts, and the three of us drove to Kincaid Park to meet Sue's riding group. Sixteen people had gathered in the parking lot, and they all were looking extremely fit and well outfitted. Sue introduced Theresa and me as the "Michigan girls" who were visiting, and we were greeted warmly and welcomed by the predominately female group. Sue and a few others picked a route that would loop us around the trail system, and we all started in clumps of four or five and headed off. I had logged just about two or three minutes on my borrowed bike, and as we rounded the first main corner, I gulped at the sight of a very short but steep hill. Most of my new biker friends made it up about halfway, as I did, and walked the bike up the last few feet. Then, less than a half mile down the trail, another hill loomed–this time even gnarlier and steeper. !*^%$#! Again, about three-quarters of the group walked rather than rode up that hill. On the last climb, Theresa had been in front of me and was almost hauled off her bike by a male rider who was losing momentum and balance. He actually started to teeter on his bike, lost his balance, and reached out and snagged her arm on his way down! What a prick, I remember thinking. I know Theresa was pretty pissed, but I learned that he apologized later; I was still very unimpressed that he had done that. The trail continued on to be an up and down roller, and I began to adjust a bit and improve my gear-changing transition, which really helped on the uphills. For the most part, the group was intact, and I remember embarking on a steep decline that was an old two-track with single-track ruts that served as the trail. I kept my distance from the rider in front of me as I rode down the trail and thankfully looked up in time to see the group screeching to a halt when a girl, Terri, twisted her front tire on the banked trail and was violently thrown forward off her bike. She bruised her thigh pretty badly, but, luckily, no pileups resulted. No one else fell or lost control, and I was glad to see Theresa was safely off her bike and bent over Terri while checking out her bruised leg. Theresa had been right behind her when the accident occurred and reacted quickly by slamming on her brakes and veering off the trail. Terri's boyfriend was quickly at her side (ironically, the same guy who had almost yanked Theresa off her bike earlier), along with a few others trying to assess how badly she was hurt. There was a consensus that her leg was not broken but badly bruised, and she told us that she could not ride out. While this was going on, I milled around talking with the other riders, who seemed impatient. We noted that a moose was watching us from up the hill, which added to our tension. So, the conversation swirled around who had a cell phone to call a park employee and whether the moose up the trail was going to get pissed and come down and stomp us. Fifteen minutes had passed, and a park guy showed up in a four-wheeler, but Terri's boyfriend vehemently refused this mode of transportation. He sent him back to get an old pickup truck to drive them back to our location. Waiting for the truck to arrive, Sue and her friend Mary had given up and had ridden back to the Suburban, jumped in the SUV, and found their way back to our location. I laughed as I saw them pull up and then moments later, the exasperated park employee drove up. With the help of several of us, Terri was gingerly lifted into the truck bed, and then she was taken to get checked at a local med shed. The group seemed to break up a bit, and I think after the long stall several people had given up and headed back, but Sue, Mary, Theresa, and I decided we would still get a bit of a ride in that night. We rode a trail called Rollercoaster, with Theresa and Sue in the lead and Mary and me following behind. We did see yet another moose as we rode, but we generally rode unimpeded for a half hour or more on a moderate trail without the steeps we had encountered before. We looped back toward the parking lot, and I was relieved and tired when we racked the bikes and threw on sweatshirts to fight the evening chill. I did have enough energy to join Sue and her gang at the Bear Tooth downtown for snacks and margaritas. I chatted and sipped drinks with Sue's gang and got to know them a bit, and we recalled the earlier spill and hoped Terri would be all right. No one seemed too worried, as we agreed that her loving boyfriend was no doubt by her side. I noted the tightness in my legs as I sat in the booth and sipped my drink. Paired with the earlier hike, it was time to call it a day.

I woke up Thursday and lounged in a pile of pillows and a down comforter on my bed and enjoyed a good, solid lazy sleep-in, finally. It was wet and rainy out, so I was in no hurry to be motivated for athletic activities. Over breakfast, I smiled as Theresa told me how excited she had been to enjoy a lazy morning as well. We did finally get motivated and hopped in the rented Honda and made the short drive to Girdwood and the Crow Creek Mine area. The mine was a historically preserved area, complete with panning equipment if you wanted to try your luck in the nearby river and connecting streams. I did not do any panning in the misty rain, but I did pay $3 and walked around the old restored buildings and read about the pioneers who had started the mine hundreds of years ago. Then, we followed a trail that led us down to a rushing river lined with rocks and telltale signs that it had been previously mined. The rain started coming down much harder than the previous mist, and it forced us to abandon our exploration efforts and head back to the car. We drove a short few miles to Crow's Pass, and the winding dirt road led us to a trailhead that began with a beautiful cascading river through a very rocky area. Even in the rain, I snapped some photos of this scene, but with the soggy weather, we did not continue up the river on the trail. We had planned to do a short hike at Crow's Pass, but instead we drove back down the dirt road and found Chair 5 Restaurant near the base of Aleyeska Ski Resort. We made our way inside to the rustic wood building and removed our soggy coats and secured a table near the bar. I ordered us a round of Bloody Marys to start, and, for lunch, halibut seemed appropriate—fresh caught, of course. Theresa chose the halibut blackened in a Southwest wrap, and I ordered the lightly battered and fried version; both were excellent. After lunch, we put some more miles on the rental car and headed back to Sue's to ready for our evening bike ride with our host. Hilltop Ski Area was to be our locale for riding that night, sans the 16 people from before. Just the three of us rode the Hilltop area, and it featured some fun and hilly single-tracks and a few gnarlynasty hills that gave my thighs a thrashing. The scenery was beautiful again but difficult to appreciate on a bike. Bubbly stream beds and stately spruces and evergreens lined the trail on this section. My focus though, was, unfortunately, on keeping up with Theresa and Sue, who both seemed to have found a burst of energy on this ride. We did stop periodically to rest and water, and Sue would relay stories of the latest bear and moose maulings, which gave me a bit of mental unrest on being in the back–alone! It was a very fun ride, but the bumpy rooted sections made for a very tender backside for me, still leftover from the previous day's ride. After about two hours, I was back at home base and in the shower, and then the sauna again, before falling exhausted into my pillows and comforter just after midnight.

Friday and Saturday, Kenai and Seward

With so much to see, Friday and Saturday turned us south to the ocean and the marine portion of the trip. Sue had armed us with maps and suggestions for things to see and do once we hit the southern Alaskan coast, and with backpacks in the Honda, we set off for the two-hour drive to Seward. Sue stayed behind with her two boys for this portion of the adventure. Theresa and I left around 10 a.m. Friday and headed south on the Seward Highway, past Girdwood and the Portage Glacier turnoff. Then we meandered along the highway as it followed Turnagain Arm. Around every corner, I was greeted by a spectacular mountain peak view, intersecting with the deep blue of the water's edge. Some fog and low clouds obscured the views that day, as the rainy weather from before had followed us. We stopped at a cool river gorge scenic turnout for some photos and then continued on; there were so many scenic pull-offs in Alaska that if you stopped at each one, you would never get anywhere. We continued on. As we drove, in honor of a travel companion on a previous ski trip in Aspen, Cousin Roger, we enthusiastically proclaimed in turn, "It's gorgeous, girls!" This saying was Roger's mantra and favorite line whenever he took in a gorgeous sight, which was often in the Rocky Mountains. I'll never forget it, and it seemed such a perfect thing to say as each magnificent vista presented itself along the way. We drove through tiny little towns such as Moose Pass and Snow River and then onto the outskirts of Seward and the Windsong Lodge, which would serve as our sleep quarters. I threw my bag in the room after a quick inspection, since we were both excited to see Seward and Resurrection Bay. It was a beautiful and charming harbor town that was bordered by a magnificent fjord and ocean bay. We drove into town and parked near the small boat harbor set against the cliffs and outcroppings that lined the whole marina area. Two large cruise ships were docked just down from my vantage point in another area of the main harbor. The weather had not improved, and it continued to rain and became even colder. I think it climbed to 50 degrees that day, but it was quickly plummeting with the cold rain, so jackets and stocking caps came out quickly. After adding some layers, we walked down the harbor lined with offices for fishing and tour charters. At our tour office, we collected tickets for the 3 p.m. start to a wildlife and glacier dinner cruise. With a half hour before boarding, we decided to scout around for available halibut fishing charters for the next day's activity. We settled on the Saltwater Safari Co., which had spots left on a small six-pack boat. Eagerly, both Theresa and I booked our spots with a down payment, as we were excited to get rolling on the evening cruise. Also, we found a deli for a very late lunch and ate some pasta salad while enjoying great views of the harbor. We combined our stuff into one bag for the cruise and checked for warm coats, hats, gloves, and a camera. Our boat was ready, and we walked the plank to a 100-foot cruising yacht for a six-hour adventure. The weather did not improve, but my sprits were not dampened with the prospect of seeing the bay, the fjord, the ocean, and its creatures.

Theresa and I grabbed a seat in the front that overlooked the bow, but we stayed inside since the rain was falling again. We listened to a quick speech from our captain on our plans and some safety dos and don'ts onboard. The captain piloted us and the ship out to the bay, and in just 20 minutes, we slowed and encountered a group of sea otters, which we learned were quite promiscuous in their behavior. I watched and they made me laugh as they swam on their backs and constantly washed themselves with their paws–umm, they were probably not paws, but I'm not sure whether they had arms, either! As they did this, the otters rolled over each other and on top of one another in a frisky and playful display. As I watched these playful and carefree creatures,

I forgot the cold, and we continued spotting pods of sea animals. The captain would slow the boat and allow us all to come back out on deck and gawk. This next time, it was a group of porpoises (cousins to dolphins, I learned) that made an appearance alongside our boat. The porpoises would race alongside us, then jump to the surface in a flash, and then dive out of sight. I was mesmerized by their speed and realized I would have no chance of getting pictures. I learned they were sociable and that they responded to whistles and calls. They seemed to leap out of the water almost on demand to everyone's delight. Porpoises resemble dolphins, but they are black, with a silver/gray streak, and are equally as elegant, sliding in and out of water. The captain moved us forward to the mouth of the bay and to the gulf, which meant rougher seas. The porpoises raced us for a bit, and I watched while my cold hands gripped the railing. The swells continued to get bigger as the captain found several spots to stop for some whale watching. I should mention that among the group of people on this cruise was a boisterous group of boys–an entire high school baseball team, who exuberantly rode on the front deck. They wore only jeans and T-shirts in some cases, even when we picked up speed and headed out to other parts of the bay. Everyone else stayed in as we clipped along toward the mouth of the ocean and bounced off the rising waves, but the boys held their thumbs up to the captain, indicating they wanted him to go faster. They hung onto the front railing and braced themselves for each thump as we crashed through the waves. After a few minutes, the captain, over the intercom, asked them to come in, but his pleas were met with more cheering and jeers to go faster. As if to oblige them (and teach them a lesson), the captain did indeed push on the throttle, and we went quicker through the waves. He steered the boat into a wave, and as I felt the slight turn, the boat rose and then fell sharply, bringing the boys to their knees in a violent jerking motion. They were barely able to hold onto the soaked railing, and after getting their knees whacked against the deck, they humbly joined the rest of us inside the main cabin area.

After that scene, someone spotted an orca (known as a killer whale), and we learned they travel in pods. Again, it made for difficult picture taking, but I was content to watch the orcas slide in and out of the water, with their large sharklike fins. The much larger humpback whales became visible at a farther distance; the remnants of the mist from their water spouts were visible in the air. Our group was lucky enough to see a humpback breech, as it broke the surface and then descended again dramatically into the sea. The whales were the most amazing thing to watch, I thought, as I considered the other animals I had seen so far. As we rounded the corner of the bay, after 20 minutes of whale watching, large groups of Steller sea lions lay on flat sections of rock outcroppings at the mouth of the surging waves. Huge waves crashed on the rocks and seeped up to the sea lions, who lounged unfazed by the angry seas. The boat idled in this cove for a bit, and farther down, a solitary sea lion was perched high on a rock, surrounded by hundreds of birds. I cannot remember most of the bird species and names, except for the puffin, an impressive and large diving sea bird. While we watched the sea lions, the crew informed us how lucky we had been to see so many whales, especially the humpback breeching. One humpback was seen splashing his pectoral fin several times, and we also encountered them again on our return voyage. We moved on and entered into another inlet or cove area for some glacier viewing. Since we were in the ocean en route to this new fjord, we passed through some impressively nasty waves. As we reached much calmer waters, the crew prepared and served us dinner in the large inside cabin. We dined on grilled salmon, rice, and a green salad. The meal was pretty good, and so far no one was afflicted with queasy stomachs or any loss of appetite. After dinner, the glacier came into view, and as our boat approached, I saw and felt ice chunks hitting the hull. I had a flashback to the scene in Titanic but was pulled back to reality when the captain assured us that the boat had a special hull to handle the impact of the ice. We pulled to within a quarter-mile of the glacier, but it seemed by my perspective as if I could reach out and touch it. It was massive, at about 300 feet high and several football field lengths wide. Our group had all assembled outside on the boat's front and side decks to view the sight, and we were lucky enough to see several large chunks calve and fall off into the fjord's 42-degree water. As the glacier calved, it made a thunderous crash, and I watched the tide and its ebbs and flows in this glacial bay area. The tide seemed to move circularly, and we all stared and watched nature at work for well over half an hour. It was bitterly cold, and the rain continued, so I decided to add gloves and a ski hat—aah, summer in Alaska. As we readied to leave the glacier area, I marveled at its icy blue color. We moved through the frigid seas back the way we came, and most of us settled back inside since the rougher waves would hit us again as we rounded the bay and met up with the ocean currents. The captain asked us all to sit down and hang on, and he told us that we were about to experience some above-average swells. Keep in mind that we were in a 100-foot cruiser, but as the 10–15 foot swells hit us, we were tossed about like a toy for a long 5–10 minutes. It was wild—waves crashed over the bow and into the side view windows, which made it seem as if we were being totally engulfed by the waves. I held on with a slight lump in my stomach as our hull rose up sharply and then crashed down through the next swell. I think some of my travel mates thought it was fun, but I tightened my stomach in anticipation as each huge wave hit us. I started to think about what it would be like in a small halibut fishing charter boat in seas like this, and I began to panic about my decision for the next day.

I continued to think this over on the return ride, which took about 1 1/2 hours. That time was broken up by whale spottings, sea otters, and a bald eagle sailing above us near the rocks. Overall, the evening cruise had been awesome, except for the spurts of rough seas. Once back at the dock, Theresa and I decided to belly up at a local bar called Christos for a beer. We each had just one and then found our way back to the lodge. En route, we both admitted how we were feeling about the halibut fishing adventure the next day. We sighed and laughed about "turning chicken" and were so happy that we each felt the same way! It was decided that we would abort the fishing mission. After the day's rain, cold, and extra-large waves, the thought of being tossed about in a much smaller boat did not sound inviting. We agreed that our seven hours out to sea that day would suffice for our maritime sightseeing. Of course, the fishing charter office was closed at that hour, and it looked as if we were out the $185 each, with no refund. I did call and left a message on their machine to let them know we were canceling and asked whether we could transfer the fee to our friends Sue and Earle to use at a later date. I think we were both relieved to go to sleep that night not thinking about being tossed around on rough seas. My halibut fishing would have to wait. The lost money smarted a bit, but as time passed later on the trip, I realized I had made a good decision. I laid my head down on the crisp white hotel pillows and wondered how I would choose a favorite part of this trip.

Only one more day in this great state, I thought, on the last morning. For the second time on this trip, I slept in lazily, and my hungry friend, Theresa, started pressing me to get moving to find breakfast and coffee. In lieu of fishing, over coffee we decided to make a visit to nearby Exit Glacier and then take a hike following a river also close by. Exit Glacier is the tourist trap of glaciers in Alaska because of how convenient it is to park and then walk up an easy trail to within yards of this shrinking mammoth. Even so, I was enthralled to be so close to this monster of ice, and I walked all around its perimeter and posed for photos by the caution signs warning people not to cross boundary lines. A melting or calving glacier is a very powerful force of nature and certainly could cause great harm, or so the posted signs said. The sun shone very brightly that day, and I could also hear the glacier "talking" to us with groans and subtle cracking or splitting noises every once in a while. After taking many pictures of the glacier, we eventually moved on just down the road and found a trailhead to follow along the river. It was easy-going and generally flat, with the only worries being a marauding grizzly or a moose in the rut. Luckily, we did not see either but walked a bit and then lounged near the river and let the sun shine on our faces. I lay flat on my back with my head propped up on a flat stone and absorbed the warm rays and munched on some trail mix. I really focused on that moment of quiet with closed eyes, and I listened to the river running over rocks and lost myself for a moment or two. I brought myself back from that reverie and sensed that Theresa had done much of the same for that little bit of time. She and I both slid our backpacks on our shoulders and walked back to the Honda for the beginning of a journey back home.

Photos top to bottom:
Laura practices a yoga "tree pose" while overlooking a perfect view of Cook Inlet; Celebrating a climb to the top of Bird's Peak with a fist pump; Laura bonds with Sue's Chesapeake Retriever, Buster on a hike; A non-fatal encounter with a bear inside the Long Rifle Lodge and Restaurant.

CHAPTER 7

PC Powder
Park City, Utah–February 23–28, 2007

Our group: Steve Reschke, Kim Hirai, Jeff and Laura Lauinger, Theresa Hegedus, Deb Mertz-Hulverson, and me

Lodging: Canyons Resort Red Pine Condos, Y7 "Cabriolet-In and Cabriolet Out"
(almost "Ski in and ski out")

Making Plans

As I was thinking of how this trip and this group of people got organized, I realized that it was almost a two-year planning process. I think it started with Steve and me chatting about taking the lead and organizing a fun group of people to go out West and ski some real mountains. In January of 2006, we tried to coordinate dates, and our schedules did not work, but we promised to try again for 2007. By starting the process earlier, the group began to take shape and grew to seven of us. Steve volunteered to search for lodging, and we picked dates that would work for everyone. Most in this group were connected by athletic activities; Steve, Kim, and I met playing beach volleyball, and the rest of the group met through various soccer leagues, women's or coed. We all seemed to fit together by our mutual love of skiing and being active, and, of course, socializing and drinking beer were important pastimes to all of us as well. Besides, aren't all ski trips just as much about the après as the ski?

February rolled around, and we all talked excitedly about our plans. We booked flights, and Steve e-mailed snow reports as a tease for the real thing to come. Right before departure, the Lauingers got conned into buying discounted lift tickets for all of us. The task fell to them on the basis of the fact they had the earliest flight in and the ski shop with the sweet deals stayed open only until 9:00. Jeff charged more than $1,000 on his credit card for lift tickets that day, and over the course of our trip, we all handed him wads of cash or promised checks upon our return to pay for our lift tickets. I guess that was the price the Lauingers paid for being early. Meanwhile, travel days are many times riddled with unexpected delays, and Kim and Steve were the unlucky recipients of just such a thing. Their flight from Chicago Midway was delayed or cancelled, I can't remember which, so they frantically rebooked out of O'Hare and had to drive across Chicago in record time to make the second flight to Minneapolis and then onto Salt Lake.

None of us had managed to book the same flight itinerary, so Theresa, Deb, and I were traveling together, and though we escaped delays out of Chicago, we did experience an adventure of our own on the descent into Salt Lake City. While descending, we had been watching the movie The Prestige and were riveted to a tiny 20" screen hanging down from above the aisle in front of us. Our concentration on this little screen must have been a bit too intense, paired with the slight turbulence as we came over the mountain range. Almost simultaneously, the three of us reached for the air nozzles above our heads to cool the cold sweat and nausea that swept over us for the last 10 minutes of the flight. I tried to "yoga breathe" and pulled and pushed breaths in and out to focus on anything other than how queasy I felt. Luckily, I only thought about searching for the barf bag and pushed the notion out of my mind to avoid throwing up. "Use the power of The Secret," I thought, desperately needing some positive thinking, which reminded me of the bestselling book I had just read. When the three of us finally marched into the terminal, we noticed that several other passengers looked as green as we did, and they, too, stopped for water. We all ambled slowly toward the baggage claim and collected our wits as we went. While waiting for my bags, I called Laura. She and Jeff had made it up to our condo and were about to head out and do some grocery shopping for us. As the second phase of our group of seven, the three of us girls, collected our bags and skis, and I called Peak Transportation and arranged for our shuttle to pick us up. We walked outside loaded down with luggage, and an aquamarine Escalade pulled up curbside with white vinyl letters on the back window proudly displaying "Peak Transportation" with their phone number. Not exactly the passenger van shuttle I was expecting, but I had no problem riding the 45 minutes up to Park City in a pimp mobile with one of PC's finest ski bums at the wheel. We were greeted by wet roads in Salt Lake City and then snowy roads as we headed up the mountain. Deb, who sat up front, tried to relax after our flight but was greeted with fast-paced turns and high-speed traverses of I-80. We did make it to Red Pine Condos safely and joined Jeff and Laura there for beverages and some snacks. As we chatted, we learned that the final phase of our group, Steve and Kim, was going to be quite late, so we claimed beds and rooms and changed into pj's. We all agreed the condo was not as spacious as it looked online. Of course, the other benefit to arriving early was securing the only bedroom with a door and connecting bathroom. Very smart, Lauingers! The other two rooms were in the loft upstairs, open to the living room below, with a shared bathroom. As we all learned over the course of the next few days, seven of us in that space was a bit cramped, but we made do and enjoyed each other's company (well, for the most part).

It was getting late, so Deb and Theresa claimed beds, which we determined were "Everest beds" because of how high up the frame and mattress were, perched on a custom-built pine frame and headboard. I joked with Theresa and Deb that they both would need a running start to get into bed. I'm pretty sure this comment is what spawned a lengthy laughing attack brought on by Deb's infectious laughter. The three of us giggled upstairs in the loft like sorority girls, and I just waited for the probability that Laura would come up and spank us for being so loud. Our laughter finally faded, and the condo became quiet, except for the snowplow truck that seemed to pass by our window about every 20 minutes or so, scraping snow off the road. I think it was around 1:30 in the morning when travel-weary Steve and Kim finally arrived. Sleepy eyed, I heard them fumbling with the key code, so I walked downstairs and let them in. They both looked very relieved to have finally made it. They tossed down their boards and bags, and I pointed up toward the loft, to their room adjacent to the three of us. After that, it was hard to sleep for several reasons, including the plow truck scraping the pavement on the road below us and the excitement to get out on the slopes. I finally closed my eyes, and I remember being thankful that no one was snoring as I drifted off.

The Canyons and Catwalks

My next memory was around 7:00 the next morning and the smell and sound of coffee brewing in the kitchen below. Our resident morning person proved to be Laura L., and she took the lead in the mornings and made coffee and breakfast. I lazed about under the covers and listened to the sounds of breakfast and conversions in the kitchen, and I realized that most everyone was up except for me. Everyone milled about excitedly, chatting about our upcoming day between bites of cereal of gulps of coffee and pulling on layers of long underwear. I think everyone has a morning routine, and I learned a few habits of my condo mates throughout the duration of this trip. We did a pretty good job of sharing bathroom, toilet, and mirror space, but we did encounter a few funny moments in the routine of getting ready to head out each morning. Deb's habit was to dress first and then sit on her bed and use the closet mirror to very meticulously braid her hair and put on her makeup. As she was doing this the first morning, Steve walked around the corner, with a smiling and unbelieving look on his face, and said, "Deb, are you putting on makeup?" To which she replied with a flat tone and disgusted look on her face, "Yes, Steve, and you don't know me very well!" I started to giggle at this exchange and continued to rummage through my ski bag with a grin on my face. Most of us girls did not spend much time putting on makeup in the morning, but, then again, we did not look quite as polished as Deb on the mountain, either, so to each her own!

As we had arrived the night before in phases, we left in groups to head up to Canyons base and the main gondola. Our day started with blue skies and sun, and we were lucky, as it remained that way for us all day. Deb, Theresa, and I stuck together that morning and were the last to leave the condo. We rode for the first time the cabriolet that we had watched coast by our window that morning. The cabriolet was a gondola-style lift that transported you from the main parking lot and lodging areas up to the main base at the Canyons, where you could then access the ski area. Steve, Kim, Jeff, and Laura, who were ahead of us, rode up the gondola. Laura L. sent me a text message about where they were skiing and which lift they had taken. This would prove to be our method of communication on the mountain, as we all got separated quite often. The Canyons were a blur that morning of riding lifts and searching for some open runs and territory that was not jam-packed with people. The three of us scanned the trail map for better runs other than the narrow catwalks and traverses that had dominated our morning. I really should not have complained, as the scenery was gorgeous and the bright blue sky and sun were all around us on the mountain. On the trail map, we went right to left and kept moving toward the recently added terrain called the Dreamcatcher and Dreamscape lifts. Along the way, we met a friendly local who snapped a picture for us and suggested a few runs not to miss. The three of us missed the rest of our group for lunch, as there was no easy way to return to the Sun Lodge from our current position on the mountain. We continued on in search of better terrain and some lunch. Around 1:00, we stopped for lunch and waited in a horribly long line to get a hamburger and a Gatorade from a tiny log cabin that served as Dreamcatcher's "lodge." Hundreds of people sat on the few tables that lined the area, and most of us stood or sat on the snow to eat our lunch. We did manage to reconnect with our group by 2:00 and skied together in a pack for a few runs. Then we took a long, winding run called Harmony back toward midmountain. It was generally harmonious skiing and boarding under sunny skies, but Steve had a "run-in" with another boarder coming over a bridge on the way down. They collided pretty hard, but he managed to dust off and continue down the run to meet us again. Other than Steve's incident, Harmony was my favorite run that day.

Most of us headed off on various runs for the rest of the day and met at the base of the hill at the main lodge for refreshments. Sunburned and windblown skiers packed the bar, and our group scouted for a table while we ordered from the bar. A cold beer always tastes so good after a day of athletic endeavors. After two went down too easy, I thought I had better slow down. All of the girls sat down together after commandeering a table, and Steve and Jeff stayed at the bar. We ladies found a nearby table of cute guys to flirt with for a bit, led by Laura L.'s friend Sarah, who had met up with us that day. I think it was around 5:30 when we took our leave of après-ski festivities and headed back toward the cabriolet to get back to the condo. To our dismay, the cabriolet was not running, so we all walked a long half mile, loaded down with skis and boots, back to our accommodations. The "shower scramble" started once we all returned, with everyone jockeying to get into the two showers and hopefully have a bit of warm or tepid water to wash off the day's sweat. In between shower time, changing, and a few predinner snacks, a few of us read through our hostess's restaurant suggestions, and we selected Squatters Pub as our choice for dining. Eventually, we all piled in the two rentals and set off toward Park City. Squatters turned out to be a good choice for several reasons: freshly brewed beer, tasty food, and a glimpse of a movie star, none other than Kevin Bacon! After Squatters, we all headed into downtown to the Side Car for a night cap. They were featuring a live blues/rock band that finally started playing around 10:00–but at the same time, many of our group started to fade, so we stayed for only a few songs before heading back to Red Pine. The conversations on the way home and while readying for bed all centered on which resort to ski and where Steve and Kim would go. Deer Valley did not allow any snowboarding, so, unfortunately, our group would have to split up on Sunday. I finally leapt into the "Everest bed" and listened to our resident plow truck scrape snow off the road for a bit before drifting off.

Deer Valley and SnowBird

The sun had disappeared behind many layers of clouds on the next day, and instead of sun, we awoke to clouds, wind, and flurries. The group's excitement was not diluted by the weather, and we readied and ate breakfast excitedly, chatting as we had done the day before. That morning at 7:00 a.m., as I lay listening to kitchen clatter and smelling freshly brewed coffee, I determined that there would be no sleeping in on this trip. I think Deb, Theresa, and I wondered each morning, "Where's the fire?!" as a contest seemed to exist between Steve, Kim, Laura, and Jeff to see who could get moving first and out on the hill for first tracks! Something that I have learned about Steve is that he is not a morning person, either, but on ski trips, he is the first out the door. Theresa, Deb, and I usually made it out last but were still skiing by 9:30 or so. Today, we took advantage of Park City's bus system and made the transit to Deer Valley through a series of seven or eight bus stops. The bus did pick us up right out in front of our condo, but it took at least a half hour to get to Deer Valley to check in. Starting a bit later that day was OK with me because the weather had deteriorated and it was very gusty. The snow peppered down as we purchased $75 nonrefundable lift tickets for the day. While in line, we learned that two lifts had closed because of the windy conditions at the top, and we had to stay on the eastern side of the mountain to avoid those areas. Even with the visibility and weather conditions, the lift system and runs were much more user-friendly than at the Canyons. It proved to be very easy to get to different terrain on the mountain. I started with Theresa and Deb, and we chose some "blue cruisers" to warm up and connected with Jeff and Laura at Silver Lake Lodge at midmountain late morning. In near whiteout conditions, I skied a bit tentatively at first but got braver in the 2"–3" of fresh powder that had fallen. We did not encounter the crowds as we did the day before and never waited in any lines. I remember riding up the Sterling Express lift and checking out the runs that fed to that lift. As we approached the top on the chair, the wind absolutely plowed into us, so we quickly headed down and then ventured over to Quincy and the Silver Strike lifts, which were more protected. We all made full use of the grandiose and well-appointed lodges at Deer Valley for warm-ups, bathroom breaks, an espresso, and a long lunch. The five of us enjoyed a very tasty gourmet lunch at the Empire Canyon Lodge and decided we had to continue to brave the snow and wind for a couple more hours. As I skied with the group, I learned that Jeff and Laura had no fear, loved speed, and could ski any type of terrain, and I had fun trying to keep up with Theresa, our resident "ski pro." Deb and I, the more intermediate skiers of the group, stayed together on mostly blues and avoided blacks and diamonds. I had a lot of fun right after lunch on some pretty steep blues and finally got in a good tempo of turns and picked up the pace a bit. Hidden Treasure was the name of the run we all took several times, and it proved to be just that, as it was tucked on a side hill and offered some protection from the howling wind, except at the top, right off the lift. I think it may have been around 2:00 that we all split up and Theresa headed off with Deb in tow to find some more expert terrain. I admired her patience while skiing with me, the "slowpoke" of the group. I was getting tired, so I set off on an easier route back to the base. I made my way back to midmountain and found a wide-open, easy run called Success, where I casually meandered back and all the way down. My thighs were burning, so I stopped several times to rest on my last run of the day. I wondered how Steve and Kim were doing in Cottonwood Canyon as I clicked off my skis and stacked them on a rack.

I went into the lodge in search of my pals. I ran into Deb and Theresa right away. They had just come down and were swapping ski boots for shoes in the locker room area. They said they were exhausted and had overdone it on the last two runs and had to stop several times as they hunched over with heaving breaths. After delayering and shaking off all our snow-covered hats, goggles, and jackets, the three of us meandered through the lodge's maze of ski shops and stores and found our way upstairs to the main bar area. Jeff and Laura had found a table and ordered up a pitcher of hefeweizen for us all to share. Our beer finally arrived, and we downed a few pints and shared our afternoon stories on the slopes. Over beers, we unanimously voted to make a spaghetti dinner for our group back at the condo that night. It took us a while to get back to the condo and hook up with our mates, Steve and Kim. The bus system proved a bit sluggish, and we waited for a half hour at the transfer station in Park City before a bus picked us up and delivered us back to Red Pine and the Canyons. Steve and Kim had beaten us back, and we all swapped snowy and windy "war stories" as we stowed skis, boards, and gear to ready for dinner. Laura L. and Deb volunteered to drive to Albertsons and pick up the needed supplies for spaghetti and cheesy bread. Steve, Theresa, Kim, and I shoved them out the door and told them to hurry because we were getting quite hungry. We heard later that Laura L. practically sprinted through the store as she threw things in a cart, with Deb (a vegan) stopping and reading labels to make sure our food items were healthy and did not contain partially hydrogenated oils! This seemed particularly funny because Laura's day job was as a corporate nutritionist—who apparently was on "vacation" from her job and still eating healthy! I think Deb even asked

Laura while shopping what her career credentials were! None of us minded her selections and happily munched on salty chips/snacks and sugar cereal in the mornings. Once the two shoppers returned, all five of us bumped into each other in an effort to put groceries away, boil noodles, and prep cheesy garlic bread. About an hour later, we all sat down at the table or lounged on the couch (Jeff was watching an old WWII movie featuring General Patton!) and happily gorged ourselves on spaghetti, sauce, and bread, washed down with a glass or two of red wine. While we ate, we noticed that it had begun to snow again quite heavily, and it continued to come down until late that night. We all went to bed in anticipation of skiing in powder the next morning.

PC Powder

Our third day proved to be the best conditions yet, with bright blue skies and sun and 12" or more of snow that had fallen the night before. Jeff and Laura and Steve and Kim were up early and, of course, planned to be the first on the mountain for first tracks in virgin powder! As had become the trend, Theresa, Deb, and I were the caboose, but we relished a lazy morning to sip coffee versus gulping, and we took our time getting ready. The three of us made it to Park City Mountain about an hour after our friends, but we were surprised to find that a few runs still had untouched sections of fluffy and light Utah powder. Deb and I both were new to skiing in powder, so it took a bit of adjustment. Theresa would coach us and tell Deb and me to "let them run" instead of being tentative. We all met up near the top, and I watched Kim and Theresa take off down a steep section of crisp, sparkling powder, where they carved turns into the snow and avoided protruding trees and bushes. I stayed safe on the traverse, and around the bend, the trails converged and fed into the same lift.

We all managed to stay together through the late morning, but I found myself following our group and then off the lift, only to stare down a butt-puckering, steep black mogul run with no other way down.

Shit! From this position, I also watched skiers hiking up around a ridge to ski in the diamond bowls next to a run that I now stared down called McCoskeys. I know Theresa noticed Deb's and my panic, and she was nice enough to talk us down the first steep section until we could get our bearings. Basically, I slid down each mogul very slowly and panted after each three or four turns, and, finally, things leveled a bit and I realized I was on my own because the others had gone ahead. I started down to finish the run and fell on my side twice while navigating the bumps, but I collected myself and skied straight ahead to a restaurant for a bathroom break. I had lost all sight of my crew, so I thoroughly studied the trail map to avoid the run I had just come down; I found a trail that brought me back to easier terrain and skied alone for while until it was time to meet up for lunch. The gang trickled in for lunch as they found their way to the lodge near the Silver Lode Express lift. Apparently, I had worried some in my group when we got separated on McKoskeys; they had waited a bit and asked a few skiers whether they saw a downed skier in a blue coat. I assured Laura that I was OK, and we ate lunch in a packed lodge and all set back out pretty quickly to take advantage of the perfect conditions. Deb and I skied together that afternoon and found many great runs that fed into the King Con lift. We also found some untouched powder in a few areas running under the chair, so we had fun navigating between some small trees and back out again onto the main run. I traded my goggles for sunglasses and basked on the chair rides in the sun. Deb had taken off down a run called Sitka, with me following, and I missed how she fell, but I looked up in time to see a ski and pole some 20 feet above her. I was able to ski down and collect her gear and bring it to her. After Deb got her ski back on and we started off again, it was determined that we were both getting tired and our form was suffering as a result. After a quick stop at the lodge to pee, Theresa was just coming down a run and found us around 3:00, so we set off together to make our way back to the main lodge. Right about at our average, we were sipping Bloody Marys by 4:00

with the gang at Legends Bar & Grill. The Bloody Marys were tasty and featured gigantic stuffed olives; both Laura L. and I fought over the extras from Theresa and Deb. While we sipped, we could see from our vantage point remnants of the SLC Olympics: large vertical signs and banners bearing the Olympic logo lined the main lodge leading out to the mountain terrain. Taking turns, we recounted our day and swapped stories of the afternoon runs and reveled in all our moments in fresh powder.

Slightly buzzed, Theresa, Kim, and I stayed behind to do a little gift shopping while everyone else headed back for showers. Most of the shops at the lodge were pricey, so all I found were stickers for my sister's and brother-in-law's snowboards back home and a coffee mug for my mom and dad. We did try on a few items, including Theresa, who tried on a sweet Descente ski jacket (white with black leather trim) that was tagged at $540. We moved on in search of lower prices. In downtown PC, I finally found a few clothing items for myself and for my friend Lynn, who was dog-sitting for me. The three of us walked a bit longer, and after stopping at an ATM for cash, we drove back to Red Pine in hopes of taking a warm shower. I finally took advantage of the outdoor hot tub once back at the condo. In stages, three or four of us walked the short distance for a soak to soothe our sore quads. I am sure it was funny to see how fast three girls could strip down to a suit and jump into the tub. The soak was awesome, and we chatted with a few handsome guys who were also vacationing in PC on a ski trip. Eventually, we all made it to Davanzas Pizza for dinner, a suggestion Kim had found while walking earlier downtown. Davanzas was a casual local joint with hundreds of beer cans and bottles that lined one entire wall, top to bottom. To cover everyone's tastes, we ordered a veggie pizza, a meat lover's, and one in between with pepperoni and mushrooms. While our pies baked, pints of hefeweizen arrived lemon wedged, which we happily sipped while eating cheesy garlic bread. The three pizzas arrived 10 minutes later, and we all agreed that they were very good. I remember telling childhood stories over dinner, which evolved into the worst family vacation and camping trip stories. By my recollection, I won that battle of stories with my summer trip story, the one where I was forced to visit PTL and Heritage USA. I think this brought tears to Steve's eyes, and everyone laughed and agreed they could no longer complain about crappy camping trips with their parents! Deb took a solid second place with her story about her dad not allowing her to be late for the bus in high school. She described an incident on a fateful morning. With a curling brush stuck in her hair and her dad's bellows that the bus was waiting, the brush was abruptly cut out of its place with a large pair of scissors. The hasty cut left a jagged line in her hair! Yikes. Don't we all have a memory from growing up that haunts us still today just a little bit? Anyway, we drove back to the condo in brisk Utah night temps and checked the weather for the next day, which looked quite ominous. The lights went out around 11:00 because we all were tired.

A Freakin' Blizzard

The Lauingers had to leave us this morning because they were booked to head back a day earlier, so just Deb, Theresa, Steve, Kim, and I remained. We stayed in the midst of a freakin' blizzard! The snow from two days before paled in comparison to the sideways snow dumping that greeted us on Tuesday morning. Deb also was departing later that day, so her plan was to ski a half day and then rush back to the condo by 1:00 and shuttle back down to the airport. Extra layers were put on by all of us as we watched wide-eyed the whiteout conditions that engulfed the gondola on the ride up the mountain. We were part of the brave few (mostly locals) who chose to ski or board in those conditions. The three girls were separated from Steve and Kim, so I did not learn until later in the afternoon what had happened to them. On their first journey up, the wind was pushing the gondola pretty stiffly and must have caught Kim's board, which was stashed outside on the racks. The wind lifted the board like a sail, and it came up and out and tragically disappeared in a poof below and started sliding down the mountain! During the next two hours, both Steve and Kim tried to recover her board and inform ski patrol, and Steve even braved the "closed run" where he knew it had fallen to try to find it. Eventually, ski patrol contacted Kim at the lodge, where she was marooned, and sent her board up to her!

While that fiasco was going on, I skied in 12"–18" of powder on runs I could barely see with Theresa and Deb. We just had to laugh at the absurdity of skiing blind, especially when we were just learning to ski in deep powder. I had good moments and many silly falls getting stuck in the powder and landing in a pile of snow. Both Deb and I giggled as we pulled ourselves up and dusted off each time, while an ever-patient Theresa led the way down the hill and navigated us to open runs. On many runs I saw absolutely no one coming down, and I had to squint at the barely visible signs lining the edge of each run. We were suspended in an impenetrable cloud of white and finally took a hot chocolate break and shook our heads at the crazy weather. I have to admit that it was fun and frightening all at the same time to ski in so much snow, but the limited visibility made me nervous.

We never found Steve and Kim, and around 11:15, we all agreed to take one last run and call it good. We skied down and realized that the lodge was a short walk up and over a ridge, so Theresa and Deb started back up a two-seater lift because they figured we could take a short ride up and ski right down to the main lodge. I reluctantly followed them, and within a few short minutes, I realized my mistake as we "turtled" slowly up the hill and were pelted by snow and wind. I yelled up to them in front of me, "Where are we going, Theresa?" at the top of my lungs to make sure she could feel my exasperation to have to endure this long lift and then a long run back down again! Doc's Run finally took us all the way back down, and I took my time coming down, still feeling uncomfortable skiing through huge piles of pushed powder. At the bottom and with skis off, Theresa and I gave Deb a quick hug and sent her off to catch her flight that afternoon. The two of us then walked down to Smokies for lunch and watched the snow pile up around us. I left a wet puddle on the bench where I had left my hat, gloves, and goggles to thaw out. With my hat off, I pushed my matted wet hair away from my face and munched on ribs and mashed potatoes. We both determined that we were done for the day and after lunch returned to the condo via the cabriolet and happily relaxed for the afternoon. With the condo devoid of most of my travel mates, I curled up on the couch with a blanket and took an absolutely divine nap for over an hour! I think Theresa was reading, and in my half doze, I caught highlights on ESPN and eventually pulled myself off of the couch to check voicemails. By 2:00, the snow had lightened considerably, and the storm appeared to be breaking. I figured that Steve and Kim would be showing up around 4:00, so I lazed around watching TV until they made it back to tell us the story of how she lost her board, getting blown out of the gondola. The four of us chatted about how crazy the conditions had been, and Kim recounted the details of how ski patrol had finally collaborated to find her board and get it to her. I think some of the Canyons staff had given up and told her it would be the spring thaw before she would find it. Steve filled us in on their afternoon, and, right after lunch, the snow lightened a bit and the last two hours of the day were the best–of course when I was taking my nap. But, I thought about it and decided I did not want to trade my nap!

Our group had dwindled from seven to four, but we made use of the now spacious condo and moved stuff into the vacant room to spread out a bit. The "final four," as I called us, showered up–all with hot water! Yeah! For dinner, we drove into Park City and found a locally famous spot called Grub Steak, where we enjoyed a good bottle of red wine with our baseball steaks and entrees. We toasted to our adventurous four days, to good friends and laughs, and to the next trip in 2008! Cheers!

Photos top to bottom:
Laura with Deb and Theresa
at The Canyons in Park City on a
sunny day on the slopes;
The Lauingers pose with Theresa
and Deb at Deer Valley on a very
blustery day; Laura attempting to
ski in a blizzard with near zero
visibility--nice form!

CHAPTER 8

Meet You at Picchu
Peru, South America–Oct. 31–Nov. 8, 2008

Introduction

If you have ever crammed for a test, then you'll know the feeling I am about to describe–except I was not cramming for a test or for a grade but for a vacation: cramming to learn Spanish in two months and cramming to get three weeks of work done in just one. That feeling of total mental exhaustion I felt while preparing to take an exam back in college, many years back ... I felt that same pressure before finally boarding the plane in Chicago bound for Miami and then to Lima, Peru, our destination for this adventure!

Once in my seat, I let out a long exhale in my uncomfortable "no lumbar support" seat and wondered, "Did I forget something? Did I leave everything organized at work? Will our flights be running on time?" My companions, Steve and Theresa, had been using the term "peaking" to describe our excitement leading up to our South American adventure. We had all sipped a Bloody Mary at Chicago O'Hare to toast the beginning of our trip and also clinked glasses in honor of Kim (my good friend and Steve's girlfriend), who could not join us. The three of us had driven to Chicago for our send-off point, and then we would head on to Cuzco, Peru (the Katmandu of South America)–our ultimate hub of adventure. From Chicago, the next stop was Miami, then a red-eye flight at midnight to Lima. We actually traveled on Halloween night on this trip, so it seemed kind of odd, considering that I would have normally been at a Lauinger costume party in Spring Lake. As I settled in my seat on the first leg, I gathered my iPod, my Spanish phrase book, and a crossword puzzle book to help me pass the time. The two math nerds (Steve and Theresa) to my left were doing sudoku puzzles. We were ready for takeoff.

November 1, Sabado

Don't you love flight itineraries that span two days?! Just after midnight, from Miami we embarked on a five-hour flight to Lima. I watched in amusement as Theresa settled in her seat with a full-body blow-up pillow complete with eye mask. I looked over in her direction periodically, and she seemed to sleep uninterrupted. Unbelievable! I slept on and off, and I know Steve didn't get any sleep at all. We arrived on time in Lima, but I was in a sleepy daze as we passed through a myriad of lines for customs, bag claim, and an airport fee kiosk and then back through security again. Very hurriedly, we checked back in for the short flight to Cuzco, since a spirited attendant suggested we could make an earlier flight. She rushed us into another lane and said, "You hurry, and go now, now!" So, in a bit of panic, we power walked to our gate and then to a bus that took us out on the tarmac to board. We made it with about five minutes to spare! On the plane, we put Steve by the window, which he stared out of, and he kept running his hands through his hair and fidgeting excitedly, with a broad grin on his face. He turned to Theresa and me, pumped his fist at us, and exclaimed, "We are in mother-flipping Peru!" If only I had felt more awake, I would have been more excited at that moment. Even Steve's excitement plummeted briefly once on the ground in Cuzco, when his bag was missing for a bit. But, a very helpful tourist agent name Patricia navigated Steve to the Lan Airline desk and also helped us secure a reputable taxi. About 10 minutes later, we all let out a sigh to see his bag miraculously appear from a baggage attendant who walked through a side door. Yeah! I was sipping on a café con leche and was trying to wake up. I was led out to the waiting taxi for a ride to the Imperial Hotel. The full realization of our destination was now before us: the majestic snow-capped Andes rose up around us as we bumped along cobblestone roads with hundreds of honking cars. Our cabbie's front dashboard was decorated with a mini Catholic shrine. Cuzcans walked the streets and wore incredibly bright and traditionally woven clothes. Some women walked along the street, with their babies wrapped in an Incan version of a backpack. Our taxi ride never had a hint of an "express kidnapping" that we had been warned about— we made it to the hotel unharmed and were well taken care of. After paying 20 soles for our ride, we were greeted with a cup of coca tea (yes, the same leaves that are used to make cocaine) while we filled out a form that required our passport information. We were directed up to the fourth floor, where a cozy triple room was set up with three twin beds. We arrived out of breath on the top floor, realizing that Cuzco sat at 11,000 feet, which is really quite high! All three of us collapsed on our beds for a while and contemplated what we would have the energy to do for the rest of the day.

After a short siesta and a hot shower, we ventured out in search of lunch. All three of us were starving, so we walked briskly toward what we thought was the center of town. As we walked down our street, not far from the hotel, we realized that we were staying in the "Dentist" and "Mattress" district; shops lined this street, with signs promising bright white smiles and a comfortable sleep. Tarped twin mattresses were stacked and piled up in the shops and almost spilled out onto the street–I wondered, "Did some warehouse in South America dump its entire overstock here in Cuzco?" I think I was still in a jet lag haze as we all ambled farther up the street that eventually dumped us out into San Francisco Plaza. The plaza boasted an open market on November 1, All Saints Day. We walked through the market past local vendors, some with roasted guinea pigs and piles of specialty breads. The guinea pigs had all been roasted whole, and large butcher knives were being used to sever sections for hungry patrons who partook in this Peruvian delicacy. I decided I just was not ready to take a bite of a roasted animal that may have been sitting in the sun all afternoon. Plus, the beady eyes and snouts of the roasted animals kinda freaked me out a bit. We all found the food culture very interesting, and all we purchased was a very safe loaf of bread, or pan, that we munched on as we walked the plaza. We found some carbonated water "with gas" to drink, as the aroma of guinea pig must have peaked our hunger. We continued to Plaza de Armas and tried to find a spot for a comida. We found a restaurant with the help of a young "street rep" who handed us a flyer for Amuru. As we would learn, Cuzco was full of young Cuzcans hired by various clubs or restaurants to entice tourists to imbibe at their places of business. With a broad smile, they would approach you, pass you a flyer, point you to the entrance, and then actually walk you right up to the hostess. I was pretty sure this was a straight commission basis for pay. At Amuru, we were led to a great perch on a small balcony overlooking a bustling street and the plaza. I ordered the local brew, a Cuzquena, and the special, pollo con arroz y tomato y peppers. Theresa ordered llomo saltado, with alpaca strips and veggies, and Steve downed two stuffed peppers, called rellenos. The meal was quite good, and we enjoyed the new tastes, sounds, and sights of Cuzco on our first day. There was no rush when dining there, so we took 1 1/2 hours to eat and sip our beers. After settling up with our waitress, we moved on down to the street level; back in the plaza, Steve was negotiating a good deal with a smiley young lady on a purchase of a hand-knitted Cuzcan ski cap. I think she was saying it was made of alpaca fur, but as I examined it close up, it looked like regular wool to me. Both Theresa and I snapped pictures as Steve tried on several hats, and we came to a decision on which color Kim would like best. As he narrowed in, the girl said to Steve, "Special price for you!" Actually, all three of us experienced Cuzcan shopping that day. I was enthralled with a long row of open shops that boasted sweaters, hats, scarves, belts, and a myriad of brightly colored woven items. All the items were incredibly cheap, so we all bought a few things: I bought three scarves for 20 soles, which equated to about $8 for all three. Theresa bought a white alpaca sweater, adorned with a golden tan trim and knitted fringes. Theresa and I also managed a tour of the local cathedral around 4:00 that afternoon (we could not convince Steve to go in), and inside Theresa snapped illegal photos of the well-appointed church. The artwork inside was the highlight, along with extremely ornate woodwork and carvings. One painting depicted the Last Supper South American style–with the main dish appropriately a roast guinea pig! After that, all three of us were in dire need of a nap. We walked back and crashed for a couple of hours. We actually got under the covers and slept soundly for at least two hours. We all woke up with throbbing headaches, but we decided it was best to keep moving. Still groggy and feeling really weird, I popped a Rolaids in my mouth and slipped on a pair of jeans. (I should take a moment and warn any traveler who will be staying above 10,000 feet to be prepared for some altitude symptoms–staying hydrated is the key.) We settled on again walking up the same street to the part of town we knew, and I sucked in deep breaths to try to clear my head. We had settled on a restaurant called Los Perros, which was recommended in Frommer's Guide to Peru. I would describe it as a funky, cool fusion restaurant, owned by a Peruvian/Aussie couple. The lighting was dim, and the seating consisted of couches or stools around coffee tables, with brightly painted walls and huge circular dangling lights that cast a dim glow around our table. The food was quite good. We sampled spreads on breads, olives, roasted peppers, yucca fries, and chili rolls, and we also tried a signature drink made with egg whites and pisco liquor, called a pisco sour. We continued on a Peruvian pub crawl next to a salsa dancing club and then to Ukuku's for our final stand on that night. We tried the "tourist" drink and the area's namesake, a Machu Picchu. The drink was two layers of sugary-style Kool-Aid, followed by hard booze at the end. While we drank, a seven-piece band played a salsa-Peruvian-Spanish mix, with a lovely dark-haired diva at the microphone. I truly wish we had had more energy to stay and take in the lively crowd and the music, but we could manage to make it through only about three songs before we all nodded at each other. We walked back and collapsed into a deep slumber.

November 2 (Domingo)

On this day, we would meet nine strangers who shared our adventurous spirit! I determined that the sun rose at about 5:30 or 6 a.m., so it was a bit difficult to sleep in. I remember covering my eyes at 6:00 from the extremely bright sunlight that filtered in our windows, and then I slipped back into sleep until 7:00. About that time, my roommates, Steve and Theresa, were both hungry again. We ate breakfast downstairs at the hotel's dining area. I sipped some delicious coffee and had bread with some jam. Steve had made friends with the desk clerk and was able to borrow a laptop to check e-mail so the three of us could at least send word to a few people that we had arrived and were about to embark on our adventure. Shortly after breakfast and our quick e-mails, we went back upstairs, and a bit of confusion arose. The phone rang. Theresa answered, and she was greeted with rapid and worried Spanish, to which she replied, "No hablo espanol." A minute after, Steve rang the room and explained that our 11 a.m. transfer had arrived at 9:30. Steve then ran upstairs and hurried us along and helped us pack our bags and lug them down the three flights of stairs. Once downstairs, we briefly met Rachel, our main guide, as we loaded our bags into the waiting van. It turned out to be a two-block drive for all the rush. During that time, we determined that Rachel was a cheery New Zealander, very young with a beaming smile, some nervous energy, and bright blue eyes. We set off for Hotel Prisma, and the routine of checking in and coca tea began again. The process of introductions had begun as we sipped tea and milled into the lobby. Steve met his roommate, Fred, who turned out to be pretty cool. Theresa and I would share a room. We were glad to see Steve chatting easily with Fred, and we were all relieved that it was NOT the man at the Cuzco Airport who was wearing a pink shirt, safari vest, and coke-bottle glasses! Whew! And as if in affirmation, I kept hearing Rachel saying "Brilliant!" in response to many conversations all around me. Next, Rachel led a half-hour group meeting in the lobby to cover the range of activities we would share during the next few days, and she also gave us our first "Incan surprise," as she called it. We all would be privileged to get AN EXTRA NIGHT OF CAMPING as a result of a possible transportation strike that would affect the Incan Trail, trains, and other transit services. But, before that, we would do a warm-up day and another hike, as well, she explained. Rachel led the introductions and described herself as the "shocks on a bike" to make sure our trip was fun and without any major bumps!

Our group included the following 12 people: Ann and Allan from Australia, Danielle and Carl from Montreal, Brittany and Richard (currently residing in Scotland), Katie from Ireland, Sarah from Oregon (living in California), Fred from Canada (Banff area), and, of course, the tres amigos, Laura, Steve, and Theresa.

Over lunch at Nick's Sports Bar (a tourist spot for sure), we all got to know one another a bit more. We covered the basic questions: Where are you from? How did you fly in? How long did it take, and did you get all your bags? During our chat before lunch, we learned that Katie had lived in a village in Ireland just minutes from Tully Cross near Connemara, where Theresa and her sisters had visited within the past year. I was drawn to chatting with Danielle and Carl, the French speakers of the group, who also spoke excellent English and some Spanish. Sarah, we learned, was taking some time off to travel after a nursing stint and had also hit Mexico for a month before coming to Peru. Poor Anna and Allan said they were waiting on some missing baggage but were nonetheless talkative and cheery, as all Aussies seem to be. My first impression of Brittany and Richard was that they were both quite reserved and quiet. But, I learned over lunch that they were honeymooning and were planning to exchange vows on Machu Picchu or in the jungle. I was in earshot to hear that Richard flew jets for the British Royal Navy. I was very interested to learn about everyone's careers and family details. It seemed like a great group, I decided as I munched on lunch. Everyone was smiling, except for Brittany, who was feeling sketchy because of the altitude.

After lunch was served, everyone took turns in the latrine before our group was to embark on our afternoon hike. On the way to the restroom, around a corner was a small sports bar area with several TVs above the bar. To my dismay, the Detroit Lions football game was on! Of course, Steve and Theresa could not resist the urge to check on the status and score of the game. I thought futbol (soccer) was the only sport I would see televised in Peru, not American football. After lunchtime, the clouds rolled in and the wind kicked up, just in time for our scheduled hike to Saqsaywaman, pronounced "sexy woman." Our group of 13 all walked through Cuzco together, and Rachel pointed out a few sights and gestured up to a lengthy set of steps leading to a long hill that began our hike up to the Sexy Woman ruins. While chatting with Sarah, Katie, and Fred, we ascended a long stint of stairs, through a brisk and chilly wind. I put on all the layers I had, including my raincoat, which was now serving as a Windbreaker. I stayed pretty warm, except for my fingers and hands. We met up with another guide, who began a history lesson of the ruins. After about a half mile more walking, we were treated to the first set of ancient Incan ruins made of massive 300-ton rocks that fit together like exact puzzle pieces. How and why these stones were placed in that formation is still being speculated among historians. We all gawked at the 10–15-foot-tall stone mammoths and proceeded farther up the hill to get a view from above. I tried to determine whether the structure was in the shape of an animal–or maybe its slight curves were depicting the body of a sexy woman, for its namesake. The craftsmanship was amazing, and most of our discussions and wonderment revolved around how anyone (or hundreds of people) could have hauled and placed these rocks with such perfect precision. And, of course, why? What was the significance of these particular structures? We toured around the ruins at all angles and found a spot where children were climbing to the top section of rocks and then sliding down on their butts on well-worn grooves. It was clearly a popular pastime because the rock slide had been worn smooth by countless kids' backsides. So, just like the little kids, a few of us big kids did the same. Steve climbed up and raced a young boy down the side-by-side slides, and then Theresa and I climbed up and raced each other down. We were surprised at how fast you got going in about 15 feet. At the bottom, we were met with a rather abrupt halt, when our feet hit the bottom and flat ground. Thankfully, Steve captured this silliness on video for us. After that, the three of us joined our group on a quick spelunking tour of a small cave, or underground passage, that led to an old irrigation area. It was a short but scary trip, as we were all engulfed in pitch black in a tight space for a few minutes before coming up to the surface. We headed back down after that the same we had come up. The rain held off, so we could gawk at the grazing llamas and alpacas on and very near the trail. I also enjoyed a nice panoramic vista of the city on the walk down. The word "Cuzco" had been cut into the vegetation of the hillside on the other side of the city. I enjoyed the warm-up hike, and the day wound down with a group dinner in a restaurant just off the Plaza de Armas. As I looked around at what everyone was eating, I noticed that trout was a staple, as well as spicy chicken in cream sauce and llomo saltado with rice. Over our meals, more "get-to-know" conversations ensued, and afterward Rachel did two briefings: one for Team Lares Trail and one for Team Classic. The two briefings were for the two options on the hike to Machu Picchu. The Lares Trail was a bit more rustic and led you through many indigenous cultures on the way, with fewer bathrooms and showers. Of course, Theresa, Steve, and I chose this option, and we listened as Rachel kept mentioning cold, rain, and snow and to be prepared for all three. I tried to determine whether this was a scare tactic or for real. Our evening wound down, with small pods of conversations continuing over Cuzquenas paired with bottled waters.

November 3 (Lunes)
"Bike, hike, bike, Pisac, bus, pack" or rinse and repeat.

The day began at 7 a.m. and ended just before 2 a.m. I had settled into my room at Hotel Prisma and began to organize piles of clothes on my side of the room on my twin bed nearest the large windows facing the street below. Theresa and I joined the group downstairs just after 7:00 for breakfast, and at 8:00 sharp we boarded a large van and chugged up a steep hill toward Pisac. As if by magic, 13 mountain bikes had been loaded onto a rack atop the van, and when we stopped at the crest of the hilltop, we all unloaded, and then a process unfolded of picking out a suitably sized bike, a helmet, and gloves. As I could see, the route was all downhill, and we all admired an impressive view down into the valley below. I put on a wWindbreaker since it was certain we would be going at high rates of speed down this mountain. The itinerary from Active South America had promised a "multisport" itinerary, and on this particular day, that was more than an accurate statement. Rachel gave us about five minutes to roll around on our bikes to be sure the brakes and gears were working properly, and then, quickly, we all started heading downward–no pedaling necessary. Single file, we spaced out and picked up speed, and, of course, Steve had found his way to the front and was flying at breakneck speed. My eyes widened as I passed by signs that read "Velociodad 35," thinking that I was exceeding this limit on my bike without needing to pedal. I rode my brakes pretty hard and let Theresa and Steve go ahead of me. The Sacred Valley lay below us as we rolled downhill, and a large river and huge sections of farmland with perfect rows created a great patchwork from this vantage point. We fit in a few photo breaks along the descent, and the mantra "It's all downhill" was reality on this section of road. After about an hour of this "scary fun," we arrived in the valley at Pisac. I remember two things about this town: a pay bathroom and an incredible artisans' market. For 1 sole at the public bano, you could enter and an attendant handed you a small piece of papel de bano that would only do for a number 1. Not sure how much it would cost to ask for papel de bano for solid waste removal–perhaps 2 soles? But, would just two sections cover it? South American and Peruvian plumbing and bathroom etiquette are a story in and of their own, and we all tried to follow the rule of not throwing toilet paper into the toilet. In each bano, signs reminded tourists to please dispose of toilet paper in the provided receptacle. Many of us forgot at times, as habits are hard to break, and, in the words of Ann, who exclaimed, "Shit, I forgot, but I am not goin' in after it!" After the bano adventures, many soles were parted with on gifts at the market. This market was row after row of Andean and Incan crafts, textiles, alpaca sweaters, tapestries, blankets, trinkets, ponchos, chess sets, journals, belts, and bracelets, all in very vibrant colors. I was most interested in the selection of fringed sweaters, and I started formulating a plan on what gifts I would get for my brother, sister, and mom and dad and, of course, myself.

I was ready to get out of my uncomfortable bike shorts, so I headed back to the bus and found a semidiscreet place to change. I rejoined the group and munched on some snack crackers before commencing up a long flight of stone steps that would bring us to more agricultural terraces and Incan ruins perched above the Sacred Valley. It was a hot day, and the sun scorched my gringo skin. The views were stunning, and along the route, we were treated to some fresh-squeezed orange juice by the locals who had set up a tourist mini-mart for our shopping pleasure. We all toured the ruins atop this peak, and in honor of the people who had built them, Theresa, Steve, and I did a "Warrior 1" yoga pose in front of a large stone altarlike structure. Just around the bend, the mini-mart had expanded, and I stopped to view woven belts all laid in neat rows on a blanket. While I made a purchase, I learned that poor Brittany was still suffering from altitude and had retched atop the Pisac ruins–her own type of offering to the Incan gods, I guess. Refreshed from shopping and some OJ, I got to hop on a bike again and continue down another slope that led back to the valley. We rolled quickly by llamas, alpacas, cows, sheep, and even a small local band parade in a village. Once we reached flat ground again, the van was waiting at a local hotel and courtyard, where we collected a box lunch and sat around on the ground and ate for a bit before embarking back to Cuzco. On the bus, talk turned quickly to packing and our evening leading up to the Lares Trail or the Classic Trail. After just an hour, we were deposited back at Hotel Prisma to pack and get ready to get into yet another vehicle for a long drive to the trailhead. The rest of the evening was a fast-paced blur of packing, a quick shower, stuffing items in a porter bag, including a sleeping bag and warm clothes, and rechecking each again.

The team gathered at 7:00 for pizza and our final trail briefings. Steve, Fred, Theresa, Katie, and the Aussies all drank a Cuzchena, and Rachel had brought a local beverage treat for us to try, chicha morata (a purple beerlike substance made from corn). The two groups began splitting off, and our group, Team Lares (or Team Larry's, as Steve pronounced it), met our new guide on this section, whose name was John Ceaser. He was animated and friendly, and he explained that we would all become like family in the next few days. So, I and my new family loaded our gear into a van around 8:00, and off we headed in the driving rain toward Pisac again and to our Lares Trail start. A three-hour drive turned into more than four hours, as we made a stop for supplies in a random village. I will never forget using the store's pit toilet in the back room next to a meat prep area spattered with blood, guts, and parts. The smell was so overwhelming I might have been better off to just pee behind the van in the rainy street. At least it did not matter whether I put the toilet paper in the toilet at this stop. After that departure, the road turned to dirt, and our driver lurched forward and slowly made his way over miles of switchback ruts perched precariously on ledges over a mountain pass. We all conferred and determined that the van was missing second gear. We watched Phillipe shift and search for a gear to grind us up the steep grade. I was thankful at least that darkness shrouded the narrowness of the road we were on and that all I saw was only that illuminated by the van's headlights ahead. During my four hours in the van, Ceaser sat to my right on the bench seat in the middle, and as he fell in and out of sleep, his head rolled back and forth and he kept leaning ever so close to my right shoulder. This process would repeat, and he would nudge my shoulder each time before jerking awake. Theresa, Steve, and Sarah were all amused at my experience with our new guide falling asleep on my shoulder. Finally, at 1:45 a.m., we rolled into a pitch-black parking area, and we waited about 10 minutes for our tents to be set up before we stumbled into bed. All I noticed, before drifting off to sleep, was a series of hot springs on a terrace below us and several other tents set up near our small camp of five tents.

November 4 (Martes)

It was Election Day back in the states, and we had absolutely no idea what was going on! We had no working cell phones or Internet on this trek, so we found out two days later, once down off the mountain, that President Obama was elected. I got to sleep in until 7:30! I awoke super groggy to the sounds of laughter and breakfast at the camp next to us. After an unsuccessful attempt to fall back asleep, I opened the tent's zippered front flap to reveal a beautiful river valley below us that led to a steep cliff wall on the other side of my vantage point. I also clearly saw the five hot spring pools laid out below us on a large tiered patio. After a quick fruit and pan breakfast, Theresa and I decided to take a soak in the naturally hot water while Steve and Sarah decided to abstain from the weird-smelling greenish-colored springs. It actually felt very refreshing, but we thought it best to rinse off in the nearby showers before changing into hiking clothes for the day. We did not get much time to relax, and by late morning, Ceaser was herding us toward a bridge that would take us over the rushing river and to the start of our hike. "Slowly and surely" was Ceaser's advice to us all as we walked up a slight incline alongside the riverbed. We passed a potato farmer who was cultivating his crops with a handheld hoe. Then Ceaser ushered us forward and explained that we would be camping at the Cuncani School that night. He described the day as our easy day, and I thought that was a fair assessment as the five of us slowly ascended up the riverbank that eventually leveled out. We walked among huge boulders that had been no doubt deposited there during a much higher version of this river in flood stage or from the nearby receding glacier. Along the river, we met groups of children who would walk alongside us for a bit, smiling brightly and saying "Hola!" Ceaser walked with the kids, hand in hand, and Theresa was also quite taken with the children and how friendly they were. She would kneel down and talk to them and give them snacks from her pack or crackers that we had been given earlier in the day. This happened frequently, and we also happened upon an older woman who was seated on the ground near her home. She was weaving a textile of some sort and sat with the loom in front of her, and she continued on with her work while Ceaser spoke to her in Quechua, the indigenous language in that area. As Ceaser explained to us, most people in the area spoke not Spanish but only Quechua, an ancient language believed to have been derived from Incan ancestors. We left the woman to her work and continued on as the sun started to go down, bringing shade and a chill to the river valley. I put on another layer and kept to the back of our group so I could "crop dust" without sharing my flatulence with the others. Altitude gives you gas, in case you didn't know.

It was just before 5:00 when we strolled into camp and were greeted with a Quechuan version of happy hour! Two teenage girls had carried beers and gifts from nearby and had meticulously laid them out for our review and purchase. Steve, Theresa, and I all selected a beer and paid our soles to the girls while throwing our gear and packs in our tents. We enjoyed a premeal of popcorn inside the one-room Cuncani

Schoolhouse. Before dinner, I checked out the maps, charts, and posters of Spanish verb conjugations that lined the walls and provided our dinner ambiance for the evening. We ate dinner and enjoyed special pisco sours from our cooks and kicked around a couple of very flat soccer balls for a few minutes before adding more layers to fight off the evening cold. We all soon retired to tents to perhaps read a book or, in my case, write a few notes in my journal. Much later that night, after we had all been sleeping for hours, we were awoken from a dead sleep to the sounds of whistles, yelling, and boisterous singing by a group of revelers who had just been deposited by the last bus after some type of a celebration nearby. Flashlights and headlights flashed over and across our tents, and all four of us lay awake and wide-eyed, just waiting for our tent to be trampled by the drunken fray. Nothing of the sort happened, and 10 minutes after the carousing had started, it dispersed into the night and our surroundings were transformed into complete quiet again. I lay awake for a while, listening to the sounds of the river rushing by.

November 5 (Miercoles)
"Up and over two mountain passes to Lake Ipsacacha"

This day would be double the fun of the previous day, meaning twice the hiking. We walked up one mountain pass, then down and up another, and, yes, back down that one as well. After breaking camp, we stowed our gear in bags that got attached to three or four mountain ponies, who toted all the camping necessities from one site to the next. All we pampered vacationers had to do was carry a very light day pack with snacks, water, and a rain jacket. I wish I could say I was badass enough to carry all my gear, but the other part of me actually wanted to enjoy the trip and the scenery. Besides, the trail was steep, so I was happy not to be too loaded down, especially today. Our small group had started up the ridge on this morning while talking and laughing about the midnight silliness that had us up for a bit the night before. We also happened by some beautiful yellow wildflowers that lined the trail. Ceaser picked three sprigs of yellow bouquets and told us to put them in our hair or hat. He explained that the locals would understand this to mean that we were single and available. Sarah, Theresa, and I all proudly wore yellow flowers to signify our availability that day. We kept walking, and quickly the school started to look quite small behind us as the distance increased. With our aggressive walking plans, Steve kept us all fueled with his homemade jerky and gorp. Ceaser seemed to really like the jerky, and he always made sure to be by Steve's side when it was passed around. We walked, we snacked, and we passed more llamas and alpacas. The animals seemed to choose the steepest sections of the mountainside to graze, and they looked up and perked their ears as we passed by. The heights today made me a bit dizzy; my vertigo made an appearance on sections of the hike. We rounded a ridgeline that was perched high above a pueblo below, and I just tried to stay as far away as possible from the edge of the trail/cliff. We stopped for lunch in between passes, and it was delicious, as were all the meals on the trail. Julio, our camp chef, whipped up another verdura sopa, or vegetable soup, and a plate of palta rellenas, or stuffed avocados. Super delicious. We did not have a ton of time to dally after lunch, so we were ushered forward by Ceaser; however, he did give us a break in the afternoon sun and took a minute to tell us about some Incan traditions and the Incan cross and its symbolism. We all sat with rocks at our backs for makeshift chairs and listened to Ceaser's enthusiastic rendition of the Incan religion and its gods. We learned that Mother Earth was named Pacha Mama and that a condor represented the afterlife. The condor would swoop down and symbolically take your soul upon your death to the afterlife beyond. He was an engaging speaker, but I did manage to scan the area around us and noticed a mountain lake behind us tucked in between boulder gardens scattered randomly. Theresa kept a drawing and notes on each section of the Incan cross and what each prong represented. The sun was the circle in the middle, and the upper right side was made up of three animals, including a condor, a puma, and a snake. The bottom right section reminded you not to lie, steal, or be lazy. The upper left side symbolized the upper world, earth, and the underworld. The bottom left had three areas entitled community, king, and reciprocity. Adding more layers to its meaning, the four corners of the cross each had a key city named, with Cuzco being in the center as the most important of the five. After our lesson, we kept walking and happened upon another shopping experience at our next rest stop near a tiny village. I distinctly remember how the locals would lure us into buying items. It was a brilliant spotter system. The local children, maybe 5–8 years old, would approach us on the trail and smile and greet us with a "Hola!" Then they would scurry away and on ahead to their moms and sisters, who were warned of our approach. They would have time to "set up shop" on a blanket on the ground just off the trail. It was difficult not to buy something at each of these traveling shops. The kids were incredibly cute, with huge grins and windburned cheeks. On some occasions, they would grab your hand and walk along with you for a bit. Of course, they happily accepted food from us, such as crackers, fruit, or chocolate. I bought an Incan cross necklace at the "shop" that day, which seemed perfect, considering the story I had just heard. I realized I was starting to get tired as we approached the highest point of our hike at 14,200 feet in elevation. During this section, we were enveloped in a fog, and I was panting heavily and focused on exhaling forcefully to rid myself of the bad air. The fog lifted at the peak of the pass, and we could start to make out our surroundings. On Ceaser's request, we all placed stones on top of a flat rock and then made offerings to Pacha Mama. Steve poured a bit of his pisco on the rocks, Ceaser poured a small amount of agua florita over the stones, and, to top it off, we left part of a cookie and some gorp as an offering. Ceaser gave us all a minute to have some personal time with our own gods or Pacha Mama, as we saw fit. We all drifted away to our own thoughts, and it remained quiet atop that mountain for 10 minutes before I heard steps again on the trail. We started moving back down, and my hips and knees started to ache, but I forgot quickly as I caught site of our campsite down below next to another beautiful lake graced by hundreds of alpacas grazing nearby. We slowly made our way down a very muddy trail, and our reward was another happy hour and cold beers.

That night was our coldest night on the trail, and I put on all the layers I had, along with a ski cap and heavy gloves. Thankfully, the mess tent served as our dining hall, and it also broke the brisk wind from beating on us all night. We stayed in the mess tent the remainder of the evening, and Steve taught Ceaser how to play Texas Hold 'Em poker. We played poker and hoarded our cookies, which served as our chips, while the rain came down outside. Theresa also had her iPod and portable speakers to add to our entertainment. We played for about an hour, and we usually readied to bunk down around 9:00, our mountain bedtime. Julio had given us a nightcap of fruit tea with rum, which seemed to help steer me toward my sleeping bag. The rain and wind had picked up considerably, so we hurried for our tents. The wind blew over our bano tent during the night, and the white toilet seat sat alone on the side of the hill pelted with rain. I lay in the tent as huge gusts of wind would momentarily cave in a portion of the tent on my side. I would grimace until each gust passed, and this pattern continued for about two hours. Things started to calm down, and just as I thought sleep might overtake me, I realized I had to pee. Aaahhhh! I debated with myself and fought the urge but gave up after midnight. I took only about two steps away from the front of the tent and just squatted to pee right there since the bano tent had blown over.

November 6 (Jueves)

This would be our last day on the trail toward Machu Picchu, and the four of us would walk down to the valley below and to a village called

Willoq to our pickup site. But, before embarking on our last stint, we got a rare treat and were able to take a tour of the home that lay just above our campsite. The owners had graciously allowed us stay on their land, and I would imagine that they had endured other gringos passing by en route to the famed Peruvian landmark. The home was a one-room, one-story house built with adobe bricks and mud for the main foundation and a thatched grass roof. I also learned that six people lived in that 15' × 30' space. The surroundings of the home included a guinea pig corral on the floor inside, next to a small kitchen and open fire pit. The opposite end featured the sleeping quarters, piled high with blankets and furs. To complete the décor, two fox skeletons hung from the rafters as a prize of the owner, no doubt who had caught and slain them. Ceaser spoke to the young man who sat in the home with us during our five-minute tour and thanked him for his hospitality. It was a brisk morning, and I noticed as we said our goodbyes that he wore sandals and no socks; we all had on heavy shoes or boots with thick socks. We took our leave and thanked our host, and I felt as I had before on a tour of a Tanzanian hut in Africa and realized how different living standards are from country to country. Today's walk was all downhill, and we passed more potato farms and groups of men in pods of 20 preparing the soil for planting. In unison, they all used a long, flat shovel to "bring up" the earth in nice rows and then in that same precision create a trench for planting. We also walked through a small village next to a quickly running river, and in about another two hours, we made it down trails and then dirt roads into Willoq. In a community park area next to a market building, we had lunch, of course again prepared by our chef, Julio, and the team of porters who had lugged our gear for four days. We said our good-byes to our porters and cooks: Julio, Alejandro, Saul, Poppy, and an unnamed horseman. We graciously thanked them again and handed them all a $20 bill. We all took a few extra minutes and walked through the community market, but we determined that the items there were overpriced, considering the mountaintop markets we had been shopping at. A van awaited, and I gladly hopped in to rest my feet for a bit. I learned we would take a short half-hour drive to a town named Ollyantaytambo. Ollyana was a bustling tourist destination, and as we drove into the town square, we saw an impressive lineup of shops. Internet cafés and bars lined all four sides. We were deposited in the town square, as Ceaser and his crew seemed to be trying to figure out the logistics to getting to Agues Calientes later. Military personnel patrolled the streets, and the four of us milled around and found snacks, sodas, and a café where we could relax for a bit. From the café s balcony, we watched as bus after bus of tourists rolled through. I was glad that we did more walking than sitting on a bus. Back in the main square, we met up again with Ceaser, who informed us that our 4:30 train ticket was now booked for 8 p.m., but, as a result, we were able to tour the ruins at Ollyantaytambo. I was excited at this prospect, but I already had gone several days without showering, so I desperately needed a bath and a bed, but it appeared that those luxuries would have to wait. The ruins in Ollyana featured more steps and terraces and another hour of climbing and perspiring. The Incans clearly took great pleasure in building and climbing stairs, and they were certainly not afraid of heights. The ruins there were much different and built into a cliff and mountainside. I guess they seemed the more metropolitan version compared to the Sexy Woman and Pisac ruins. Back down an hour later, I was beyond tired, and we still had to wait for our train. Ceaser led us to a hotel lobby, where we milled around and used the bano; I found a store nearby and bought a can of Pringles. I returned to the hotel lobby, and my friends descended upon me like a pack of wolves at seeing the can of salty chips. We scarfed them down and found some beers with which to wash them down. All of a sudden, Ceaser came around the bend and excitedly told us to grab our bags. We needed to go right then: he had gotten us on a 7 p.m. train, and we needed to hurry to catch it. He had found a cab for the four of us and gave the cabbie money and instructions to deposit us at the gate.

Ceaser sprinted after us, with a hotel employee running next to him with his pack, since he would not fit in our car. Somehow he made it shortly after us, grinning and out of breath. It was close, but we made it on the train. After we enjoyed our boxed-lunch meals and comfortable seats, Peru Rail deposited us, after only an hour and 40 minutes, to the famed Machu Picchu Pueblo, otherwise known as Aguas Calientes. After a five-minute walk past closed shops and over a footbridge, we arrived at Viajeros, where a lukewarm and bland dinner was waiting. None of us was very hungry, but we did eat a small plate of rice and vegetables before heading upstairs in hopes of a hot shower. Theresa took a shower first, and I prayed there would be some warm water left for me. I was thoroughly exhausted as I took my turn getting clean and then toweling off. I changed and collapsed into my twin bed and was immediately asleep. However, I was awakened by a knock at 5 a.m. It was Machu Picchu day, but I wondered why I kept picking vacations where I had to get up so freaking early! I groaned and wearily drug my ass out of my bed.

November 7 (Viernes)

Admittedly, at 5 a.m., I was not excited about much of anything. Wearily, I stumbled out of my bed and admired my swollen eyes in the mirror. I dressed and then repacked my backpack and met everyone downstairs for coffee and pancakes. I did not have much of an appetite that early, so I ate a few bites in a daze and let myself be led to a waiting bus that would take us up the mountain to the entrance. There was an option to walk up the ancient stone steps to the entrance, clearly designed for overachievers, of which I was not at the moment. Instead, I happily slouched on my tourist bus seat as the caravan bent around switchbacks and U-turns up the mountain. We were dropped off near the entrance, and a misty veil of clouds surrounded the green-laced peaks around us. The ruins were still above us, so we needed to climb another level of stairs to reach the first famous vista at this historical spot. I presented my passport to enter the park, and I paid another sole to use the bano at the entrance. Only in Peru do you have to pay to pee! After entering the park, I realized the one benefit of being up this early was that the bulk of the tourist crowd had not yet arrived. We all then ascended the steps in anticipation and hoped that the sun would start to peek out from behind a cloud layer. At the top of the staircase, a spectacular view opened up, and I took in my first views of Machu Picchu. It was misty and mysterious, I thought, as I gazed around the perimeter of the ruins built atop tall and narrow peaks that jutted up to the sky. If you get the opportunity to see this for yourself, you, too, will wonder how the Incans could have possibly built such a place in this location. We all took some "Japanese time" at Ceaser's suggestion and snapped many photos of this amazing monument. Ceaser led us to one of the large grassy terraces that overlooked the main temples and ruins, where we sat down and listened to a brief history of Incan kings, the people who had lived here, and how a man named Hiram (from the United States) led two discovery expeditions to unearth the marvel as it is seen today. I also learned that the main ruins were only just discovered 100 years ago! Wow! Ceaser, very passionately, wove a story for us, and while he spoke, the clouds began to lift and the sun shone on MP for us. It truly was gorgeous, especially with all the jagged peaks around it and behind it, essentially framing it. A true wonder of the world! We took the next two hours and walked the various levels of ruins and buildings. We admired the Incan stonework and toured the Temple of the Condor and then an Incan toilet and a quarry area, where the rocks had been honed into blocks for temples or houses. Just as our tour had started, we reconnected with the other part of our group, who had arrived through the Sun Gate with another guide. We all excitedly shared our past several days' adventure with our pals. I learned that Brit and Dick had conquered their illnesses and were planning to exchange vows at MP around noon. We were all invited to the ceremony if we wanted, and Katie had volunteered to be the photographer for them. Rachel was back on the scene also, and she told us of plans to reunite the two groups back at the hostel around 2:00 for a buffet and celebration. Next, we asked Ceaser for a pee break and went back down to the entrance. He took his leave from there and left us to explore on our own for a while. We grabbed a snack and quickly put on bug spray to detract small mites that were attacking our legs. Theresa had looked down to realize that a bunch of tiny red bloody welts had started to appear on her calves. So, we all quickly sprayed and rubbed in repellent to avoid this same fate.

The four of us voted to do some extra credit at MP instead of just standing around admiring the views. We decided to hike up to the Sun Gate to see an even more extreme view of the ruins. The sun came out in force, and sweat rolled off my face and onto the stone steps while I walked. As we ascended, the sheer cliffs got closer to the edge of the trail, so I hugged the far side of the path and averted my gaze from the dizzying heights. I was glad when we reached the top and I was able to sit in a safe spot for a bit, away from the 5,000-foot drop to the valley below. We shared this moment with Kim (who was with us in spirit) by taking a picture with a copy of her high school snapshot in the foreground, propped up on a stone window that looked out toward MP. Since she was not able to make the trip, we tried to include her as best we could in our memories. We descended on the same trail, and it was time to say adios to "Meet you at Picchu," as Steve had dubbed our destination. At the main entrance, Steve and Theresa decided to walk the steps back down to Aguas Calientes, and Sarah and I elected to take the lazy bus ride. While on the bus, Sarah panicked about Steve and Theresa's choice and was sure they would be late to meet the group and say good-bye to Ceaser. Plus, after much debate, we had all decided on a tip for Ceaser, which we had planned to give him back in town. I tried to console her, but I really was only listening to the growling of my stomach: I was hungry again! Thankfully, once back at Viajeros, an impromptu party or wedding reception for Brit and Dick was in progress. Beers were being downed with voracity by the whole group, and a very festive two hours ensued while celebrating the culmination of our hikes to Machu Picchu and the couple's marriage vows. A sweaty Theresa and Steve arrived in plenty of time to join the fun and to tip Ceaser. We handed him a wad of cash, and he said his good-byes to us as we wished him well and safe journeys in the future. With a healthy beer buzz, we all chatted about the respective trails and how different the experience was. The Classic Trail was described to be a party/bar scene after each day of hiking. We all continued to compare notes, and, still happy and buzzed, we walked up to the hot springs, or "hot pools," as Rachel called them. We took a half-hour soak in the almost hot water and downed some more beers. On the walk to and from, I took in this bustling tourist city and marveled at the sheer number of shops, hostels, hotels, and markets sporting the usual clothing items, sweaters, etc. I did do a bit more shopping but decided to wait until returning to Cuzco to buy my last gifts. Besides, we were getting pushed to get our gear organized to return to Hotel Prisma. Part 1 of our travels back was a Peru Rail ride to Ollyantatambo. On the train, we were treated to a Peruvian fashion show as the attendants donned alpaca sweaters and other fashionable clothes and marched up and down the aisle to "Dancing Queen," by ABBA, to all of our delight. Part 2 of our travels was without entertainment on a bus ride in the dark back to Cuzco, with all 12 of the group reunited again. Everyone's buzz had clearly worn off, and we were all in desperate need of a day off. Luckily, the next day was Saturday and our FREE day, as it was listed on the trip itinerary.

November 8 (Sabado)
Free day!

Sweet! I enjoyed a well-deserved sleep-in on this Saturday morning, I thought, as I languished under the covers. No deadlines, no group meetings—we were on our own. The sun shone through the curtains at 5:30, but I simply opened my eyes a crack before rolling over and falling back asleep until 8:00! At 9:00, Rachel had arranged for a cab to pick us up and drive us to Moray. Steve, Fred, Theresa, and I had decided not to sit around but rather take a little road trip. We crammed in a wagon with Brian, our taxi driver, who spoke no English. Brian drove road-rally style through the city and rocketed around turns as we headed into the more rural areas north of Cuzco. After an hour and 20 minutes (too long to be in a car, I decided, for my free day) of watching farmlands framed with snow-covered peaks, we finally arrived at the entrance of Moray. Moray is famous for its three large circular terraced ruins of agricultural significance. Steve reminded me that I was the translator as we got out of the cab, and Brian turned to me as if to wait for my instructions. In barely passable Spanish, I arranged for him to wait for an hour and then we would meet him back in the parking area and go back to Chinchero on the return for lunch. Brian nodded in affirmation, with a long string of yeses: "Si," "Si," "Si," and "Si"!

We explored Moray, and to my surprise, we actually walked DOWN a stone path and down into the circular terraces into the bottom of these craterlike creations. Once inside, as we talked, we noticed an echo, and we admired the perfectly spaced and crafted walls and steps on each level. As the history board told us, the terraces were used to plant many types of corn or potatoes—a nursery of sorts. The temperature got warmer on each level, and the very bottom was the warmest of all. Since our legs were still tired that day, we all agreed that this was the most that we could handle. At a leisurely pace, we walked back up and out of the ruins to find Brian napping behind the wheel. I tapped on the hood to rouse him, and we were off again at alarming speeds on dirt roads toward Chinchero. I leaned forward and tried my best to ask Brian a question, "Tu seis un buen restaurant en Chinchero?" He nodded and said, "Si, Senorita!" He drove us up streetside to a place and motioned for us to wait as he sprinted through the door as if to warn the proprietor that four gringos were coming! Moments later, Brian waved us in, and he also did the ordering for us as well. He asked for quattro platos de trucha con pappas y ensalada. We bought Brian his lunch for his help, and we enjoyed an open-face trout, pan-fried with the head and bones all intact. It was muy bien, we all agreed as we ate. As we sat and ate, I stumbled through another conversation in Spanish with Brian. I told him we were all from the states and where. He then asked me, "Quantos anos tienes?" (How old are you?) I replied in Spanish, "Trente nueve," to which he smiled and shook his head no and replied, "No–trente." He apparently did not believe I was 39 and said I looked no more than 30! I smiled and of course thanked him for the compliment, but I decided he just wanted a bigger tip for the cab ride.

Later that afternoon, Steve, Theresa, Fred, and I all shopped for gifts at a huge artisans' market in Cuzco. Steve wanted to find a sweater for Kim, and I finally settled on a sweater for myself and for my sister. I had started to get the hang of haggling on prices, as was the custom. You could always get a better deal than any listed price. I also found a leather-bound journal for myself and then walked around with Theresa as she tried to pick out sweaters and colors for her sisters and nieces. We wrapped up shopping so we could change and make it to the plaza near the cathedral to meet the whole group for dinner at 7:00. We had settled on Los Tomines, which was clearly unprepared for a group of 15. Service was slow, but no one seemed to mind as we sipped beers and cocktails. The highlight at dinner was Theresa's main course; she had ordered roast cuy (guinea pig). As our meals arrived, we all stopped and gawked at the rodent that was placed on her plate, complete with teeth, eyes, feet, and all. Our group was quite amused, and everyone snapped a photo of Theresa's meal as she proudly held it up near her mouth and face. Theresa sent back her cuy to be sliced so she could at least fork and knife it without needing a butcher knife to slice it into smaller sections. After a spirited dinner that lasted more than two hours, we hit the Irish pub for pints and then went on to Mythology for disco and DJ dancing. I actually ran into Ceaser while walking up the stairs into the club, so we quickly reunited and all danced in the gathering crowd to thumping Latin/dance/pop music. The music was fun, and we danced and drank for another hour. We dragged Katie out at 1 a.m. so we could catch some sleep before an early wake-up call to start our jungle portion of the trip the next day. Just before bed, I picked up my laundry at the front desk and set out a few things that I would need to pack for the jungle.

November 9 and 10
Welcome to the jungle!

I remember waking up at 6:30 to the sound of Theresa moaning from her bed. My heart sank, and as I listened more closely, I realized she was ill. She had rushed into the bathroom, and I had to listen to her expelling all her dinner, drinks, guinea pig, and whatever else into the Hotel Prisma toilet. My mind was racing: did she have food poisoning? Then, I worried whether she could handle all the logistics of the day, including bus and plane travel. So, I got up and hurriedly dressed and packed my bag while Theresa continued her offerings to the Incan porcelain god. She finally emerged from the bathroom and lay down on her bed. I realized I would need to get her organized and packed, as she was in no condition. So, while she recovered, I held up various items of clothing for her approval to pack and take to the hot and humid jungle. We were allowed to take only a small backpack for the two days into the jungle, so after getting her bag all set, I crammed the rest of her clothes, gifts, and books into her big orange duffel and set them all near the door. With all our gifts and sweaters now purchased, our bags would barely close. We would need to meet the group downstairs soon, I realized. In the rush of packing and worrying about Theresa, I almost made myself nauseous as a result, not to mention my slight hangover as well. I took a quick break and went downstairs to the lobby to refill my water bottle. I also found Steve and broke the news to him about our sick friend. When I returned to the room around 8:00, Theresa had made a bit of improvement and was sitting up and dressed. Our departure time was 8:30, so I told her to relax, and Steve went out and bought her a Gatorade to sip on to rehydrate. Luckily, Theresa tossed only one more time that morning, no doubt the result of our bumpy bus ride to the airport. She made it out of the bus doors first and decorated a taxi car's back wheel for a few minutes before recovering to make her way into the airport. Luckily, the car was empty, so no one could yell at our poor sick friend. Our whole group was obviously concerned for Theresa, especially since three people in our group had already experienced her fate. Dr. Carl stepped in and came to Theresa's rescue, with Pepcid tabs and an antinausea pill that would make her sleep.

We all had to endure airport drama at the Lan check-in with an agent on a serious power trip. Rachel did a marvelous job coordinating and finally had all our bags checked, and she handed us boarding cards. We had only an hour flight to a frontier town on the edge of the Amazon jungle called Puerto Maldonado. Thankfully, Theresa slept on the plane, and both Steve and I started to relax and realized that she would be OK. It appeared as if she would be fine in less than 24 hours. Just off the plane at 1 p.m., I stepped out into a wall of hot humidity and temperatures in the mid-80s, and an instant sweat broke out all across my body. Rachel had arranged for a bus to pick us up and take us to Inotowa Expeditions, which would lead us on our jungle tour for two days. Theresa remained sleeping on the bus, and we all got out and toured the office and rechecked our backpacks for what we would need for the next two days. Our bigger duffels would be left behind there at their headquarters. We were all introduced to two young guides, Jose Antonio and Hugo, while Rachel signed us all in on their register sheet. Back on the bus, Theresa gave me a thumbs-up that she was better, but she continued to doze while we rolled on toward the city center.

Puerto Maldonado was very rustic, and most people rode bikes up and down the dirt road we took into town to a bustling farmers' market. We all hopped out for a while and explored the market, with Jose Antonio leading the way. I admired huge displays of tropical fruit, crammed in booth after booth, and mixed in were other retail kiosks that sold videos, underwear, candy, soda, T-shirts, and many other items. We sampled a local favorite at one booth, Brazil nuts coated in sugar. The bustling market also featured several open-air restaurants and was flanked by two busy streets with bikes and motorcycles riding by. I actually witnessed an incredible sight of four people riding on one bike (two on the main seat, including one pedaling, one on the handlebars, and one balanced on the back fender). At that moment, I remembered complaining about cramming four of us in a cab on the way to Moray.

After a few more minutes in the market spent strolling around and gawking at all the fruit and nuts everywhere, we stopped at an ice cream shop right at town center that offered a bird's-eye view of two wide converging rivers. The rivers were the Madre de Dios and the Tambopata; they intersected and then ran separate ways into the jungle, both very near the borders of Bolivia and Brazil. Our group would explore the Tambopata with our new set of guides, along with Rachel, on this section of our trip. My ice cream cone was delicious, I think partially because it helped diffuse the heat and humidity all around me. Theresa was still in no mood to eat, but she seemed better and continued to doze in her seat next to a complete stranger. Back on the bus, we moved through town and past its outskirts and then onto rutted clay roads and two-tracks and over rickety wooden bridges that I was amazed held the weight of our bus and all of us. After an hour of excruciatingly slow speeds over huge bumps and potholes, I leaned out my window for some fresh air and watched us navigate over one final bridge before stopping near an open area by the riverbank. Some rustic bathrooms and a small convenience store were adjacent to our river put-in, so we all grabbed a drink and used the facilities before walking down a wooden plank to a waiting dug-out power canoesee . This long, narrow boat was more seaworthy than I thought as I stepped on board, along with all 14 of my companions. Thick jungle foliage rose up on the banks, and the noises of birds and jungle creatures filled our ears, even through the noise of the boat motor. After we all found a seat, Hugo zipped us along and up the river's muddy waters at a good clip. While he motored us forward, the other guides passed out a late lunch of rice and veggies wrapped in a banana leaf and tied in a package with a piece of string. As I opened my lunch package, I thought it was a perfect meal presentation for a jungle trip. Our boat ride lasted about 30 minutes, and I think most of us were just happy to be off the bus. I was delighted to feel the warm breeze on my face and the occasional splash of water on my arms as we moved upstream through the muddy river. We pulled up to the bank on the right side, where a rickety stairway led to a single-track trail and then disappeared into the jungle canopy. The dock and stairway were overgrown with weeds and foliage, so it was important to watch your step as you exited the boat. Jose Antonio and Hugo graciously offered a hand to all the ladies as we stepped off the boat and onto the narrow landing. The narrowness of the trail dictated that we all walk single-file through a thick green tunnel of vegetation, but after just five minutes, the canopy opened up to a large open-air lodge built about 6 feet off the ground. This would be our home for the next two days and two nights. The front of the lodge, or, rather, the porch, was a large open area with hammocks strung from the beams in all four corners. Several bamboo coffee tables were situated near the hammocks, and a large tall table along the only wall displayed skulls of caimans (small crocodiles or alligators about 3–4 feet in length), fish, piranhas, and other jungle animals. I milled around and marveled at my surroundings, tried out a hammock, and downed a glass of water as I mopped my sweat-soaked face and hair. Rachel huddled us all together and gave out room assignments. Theresa and I walked down the lone hallway that ran through the middle of the lodge and pulled back a curtain that served as our door. The room had three single beds, with jungle floral arrangements on each dresser, and long white drapes provided the only separation between our room and a step-down deck that overlooked the jungle. It was so cool and very exotic, I thought, just as this whole trip had been so far. Most of the group, including me (while Theresa slept some more), walked around the lodge for a complete tour and found the path that led to the dining area and bar. The hammocks were popular, as were the very comfortable lounge chairs. We all took this time to relax, except for Steve and Fred, whose hyperactive energy had them out walking the trails and looking for critters, bugs, and the elusive canopy monkeys. Later that night, after a dinner by candlelight, we took our first scheduled nocturnal walk. We were all armed with headlamps and flashlights, and most of us were thankful that the lodge had knee-high rubber boots that we happily slipped on. At the beginning of the walk, I developed (along with most of the group) a "creepy-crawly" syndrome that made me feel as if ants or spiders were crawling on me. Eeeeks. It was hard not to be nervous when walking around in the dark in the jungle. Not five minutes into the walk, Jose Antonio stopped the group and had us gather round a tarantula hole just a foot off the trail. He coaxed this mother tarantula out of her hole with a short stick, and she appeared to our delight, along with six babies to boot. She was an impressive creature just by sheer size; she was 4 inches wide and had thick, hairy legs. She was cool but totally creeped me out. I kept a lookout around my feet for other such creatures. I walked more nervously forward after that experience and checked all around every five seconds or so. I learned that tarantulas do not kill their prey with poisonous venom; instead, they crush it with their many strong legs before devouring it. What a nice thought to have in my head just before bedtime. Jose Antonio pointed out another tarantula along our path and also a bright green tree frog and a long and skinny stick bug attached to a large green leaf. We gawked at all these creatures and attempted to take pictures in the dark, none of which turned out on my camera. After an hour of nocturnal walking, Rachel suggested that we head back and go to bed early because we had a 4:45 a.m. wake-up call. Falling asleep in our jungle paradise was easier said than done, especially since I had the feeling that some poisonous creature would crawl from under my sheets and attack my exposed skin. So, with that thought in my head, I checked for bugs in my bed and then gathered my bed netting cover and tucked it in as tightly as possible around each side of the bed. Finally, secure enough in my cocoon, I drifted off hearing wild-sounding screeches and howls off in the dark. Sigh ... there is just no hope of sleeping in on adventure vacations. At 4:45, I was jostled awake by Theresa, who was feeling better and said it was time to get ready for bird-watching paradise. Apparently, parrots and macaws awoke in the morning at 4:30, so our group got up early as well to see the birds start the day. Half awake, we marched down the trail to our waiting boat, and we zipped along to a waiting "bird blind" to see all the birds assemble in the trees and on the clay banks. Jose Antonio and Hugo led us up a slippery clay bank to the blind and urged us to be quiet and take a seat on the wood benches. A narrow opening in the wooden blind gave us enough room to watch as thousands of macaws and parrots converged about 100 yards away. I was amazed at the level of noise these birds could generate. Several of my trip mates passed around binoculars so we could all zoom in and see this talkative and brightly colored species. We learned that the birds' diet consisted of berries and fruits, so to offset the acidity, they would eat small amounts of clay to line their stomachs. So the reason they attached themselves to the clay banks was to get their daily fill of bird antacid. Bird watching was the first of four excursions we would take part in that day. I must admit that when I got to the bird blind, I forgot the time and got wrapped up in enjoying the early-morning bird party. The next three excursions included a trip to an oxbow lake to fish for piranhas, a medicinal and Viagra plant walk, and another nocturnal adventure on the river for caiman spotting. Yes, all that happened in just one day.

The oxbow lake adventure was pretty amusing and crazy hot. We had to hike into a dock area, where our large flat boat waited for us. Our method of propulsion was a large stick (like Huck Finn) to move the large boat lazily over the water. As we slipped through the calm waters, Jose Antonio searched for wildlife to point out to us. We were fortunate to see some turtles and several bats sleeping and attached to tree trunks. But, the highlight was, of course, piranha fishingsee . With very crude fishing poles (a skinny stick about 4 feet long, with a line attached at the end), Jose Antonio baited our hooks with chunks of raw beef. We lowered them into the water to catch the fabled man-eating fish you have all heard of. At least four or five of us caught the small but aggressive toothed fish, including me! Delighted, Theresa also reeled one in, and we happily posed for pictures while holding up a tiny piranha as if we were mighty fishermen. To Steve's chagrin, he was not able to get one on his line. After a while, we all grew bored of watching the small fish tear apart a piece of beef just under the surface of the water. We moved on and pushed off toward the middle of the lake, and our guides told us it was OK to jump in and go swimming. At first, we all thought it was crazy to take a swim in the same lake as the piranhas, caimans, and giant snapping turtles. But, we were all so hot in the 90-degree temps, and after some urging by Jose Antonio that it really was OK, one by one, we all jumped in the lake from the front of the boat. I jumped in feet first and joined my friends in the refreshing water, and miraculously, we all escaped unharmed and uneaten by any creatures. The water was at least 80 degrees, but after we pulled ourselves back on the boat, our wet clothes helped to keep us cool for a little while. The sun was scorching that day, and I remembered to reapply sunscreen and wear a hat to protect my head and face. We eventually floated back to the dock and hiked back out to the river. On each of the jungle day hikes, I scanned the foliage and trees for birds and critters; it seemed important to me to keep a watchful eye. Huge termite nests clung to tree trunks, bees buzzed loudly, and intermittent "water droplet" noises made by a bird were mixed in. I wondered what that bird looked like as I listened for another water drop to fall. We headed back to the lodge for a short break before our afternoon activity, but clouds rolled in, the sky darkened, and a stiff wind whipped up as well. Our "medicinal plant walk" got postponed as the rain started pelting down and thunder rolled in. After a short delay, we all decided to go anyway in the rain. We all pulled on rubber boots that covered us up to our knees (except for Steve, who wore his sandals) and rain coats. I loved the boots because they made me more confident while tramping around near critters. Perhaps I would not be lethally bitten or stung and then medivaced out! Jose Antonio pointed out tree and plant species that were known for healing or medicinal qualities. We saw plants that provided a snake bite antidote and a Viagra substitute, and the bark of one tree smelled just like raw garlic. Weird. Our group also encountered a school of fire ants that had started to cross our trail and started climbing all over Katie's and Theresa's boots, to their panicked dismay. We also must have disturbed a bee or wasp nest near the trail, as a few angry insects bit Katie and Richard. We quickly moved forward and finally escaped the wrath of stinging insects and made it back to the lodge for a bit of downtime. We had dinner, but our group had developed a growing irritation for another family staying in the lodge and joining us during mealtimes. They had an annoying habit of stealing all the vegetables from the meal. They would pick out all the veggies without sharing or passing. We grumbled about them but fought the urge to pick a fight with strangers we would never see again. After dinner, Katie taught us a complicated card game called 25, which we never quite mastered. Theresa, Steve, and I commented that we thought that Euchre was difficult, but this game was so multilayered and strange we never figured it out. Richard commented to us that the card game was decidedly Irish, so it was unlikely to be logical or easy. Thankfully, it was time to ready for our last excursion, so we had to get up and change and be ready for caiman spotting on the river.

At 10:00 that night, we headed back out to the power canoe to try to catch glimpses of caimans. We cruised upriver, and Jose Antonio used a bright spotlight and pointed it at the banks. His trick was to look for the reflection of the eyes in the spotlight and then flag our driver to approach for a closer view. Caimans are a bit elusive, and they would slide out of view into the river or into the tall grass. We did see several from a good distance away, but we got an up-close glimpse of a white caiman on the muddy banks. Our best wildlife spot that night turned out to be not on the river but on the trail back to the lodge. We were treated to a close-up view of a three-toed sloth. The sloth hung in the canopy just above our trail. True to its name, this slow-moving creature hung in the tree about 6 feet above us and moved ever so slowly as cameras clicked and flashed all around it. After about 10 minutes of complete frenzy over spotting this creature, we finally left it in peace. I realized that I had never even heard of such an animal, so how cool was it that I was able to see a sloth! It was a great ending to our tour, and I happily went to bed and drifted off, only after tightly tucking in my bug netting around me.

The Last Day

I did get to sleep in on the last day–well, until 7:30, anyway. The day would be the beginning of a long journey home. First, I would hike, then motor by boat, and then take a bus to Puerto Maldanado airport, and then it was onto Lima for Steve, Theresa, and me. At 12:20 a.m. much later that night, the three of us would take a red-eye back to the states. Carl and Danielle were also flying to Lima from Puerto Maldanado. This meant that we would begin the process of saying good-byes to our newly acquired adventure friends. In our last hours of logistics and travels, our group exchanged e-mails and hugs and also had to console Sarah over the loss of her stolen iPod. Once at the airport, we handed a wad of cash (a big tip) to Rachel and thanked her for her cheerful attitude and guidance. I marveled at her travel and world experience at the young age of 25. I had learned in the past 10 days that she had been all over the world and survived some rather hair-raising experiences. We continued around the group with well wishes and messages of safe travels and fleeting hopes that we might see each other again. Ann and Alan invited us to join them for a Barbie in about 18 months in Perth, Australia. I also hoped there might be invitations to such destinations as Banff (Fred), Scotland (Katie), Montreal (Carl and Danielle), and so on. Steve and I had talked and wondered whether any of our trip mates were hoping to come to Michigan to visit and see the Great Lakes. After making the final rounds of hugs and handshakes, we walked out to our plane on the tarmac.

It was sad to leave the lush and beautiful green of the jungle to fly into Lima, which proved to be my least favorite part of the trip. Lima is a huge city of around 10 million people that is perched on the ocean on Peru's west coast. From the airport, through the thick smog, I could just make out the coastline of the ocean and the dingy outlines of huge freighters in port. I had imagined seeing a crisp blue ocean on the outskirts of the city, but the pollution in the city was like nothing I had seen or inhaled before. As we exited the airport, I could taste and smell why this city was enveloped in a gray cloud. Every car and taxi cab spewed black diesel smoke out of the exhaust at alarming rates. This layer of smog and fumes seemed to hang in my sinuses for days after that short visit. Thank goodness Steve had a connection, an old school friend (Neil) who lived and worked for the Peace Corp based in Lima. Steve had contacted him beforehand and had hooked up a short visit to his well-appointed apartment for showers, a few beers, and a late dinner. Graciously, Neil had arranged for his normal driver to pick us up at the airport so we could avoid the infamous car-jackings and express kidnappings. We found our driver after calling Neil, and we jammed all our luggage into his sedan and set off heading west on the main freeway. We kept driving and driving, and after 20 minutes had passed, the scenery on both sides was still the same. Dark gray and dingy hills rose up behind crowded neighborhoods, with occasional swatches of bright paint mixed in with the metal roofs and rudimentary housing. About 30 minutes west of the city, we exited and finally drove into what appeared to be a very upscale neighborhood. We unloaded and rang the bell and were led upstairs with all our bags to a very neat and contemporary apartment. We met Neil and his girlfriend and a few other friends and neighbors during our short visit. They showed us to the bathrooms for much-needed showers, and then we sat around with cold beers while telling stories of our trip and learning more about Neil's job. It was nice to relax for a bit and not be rushed. We waited to have dinner until late so we could just go from the restaurant back to the airport for our very late flight. We took an eventful cab ride to a very fancy restaurant for an exquisite meal (the only Lima highlight) called Restaurant Huacha Pucllana, which was actually located near a park of Incan ruin replicas. The five of us sat outdoors and enjoyed wine and ceviche for an appetizer and had a wonderful dinner served by a very attentive wait staff. Tiki torches burned at the corners of the patio, and, paired with the meals and other delicacies we tried, it turned out to be a good final memory of our Peruvian adventure. After paying our expensive tab and settling up with Neil and thanking him again for his hospitality, the three of us hopped in our waiting cab one last time for our journey to the airport. "Asta luego," I murmured to myself as I stared out the window back toward very fond memories of Cuzco, Machu Picchu, the Lares Trail, and also the jungle.

Photos top to bottom: Ceaser, our guide, explains the history of Machu Picchu; Laura and Theresa race down "slide rock" at ruins near Cuzco; Steve, Theresa and Laura's warrier yoga pose in honor of the Incan Gods; Hiking on the Lares trail above 14,000 feet to a campsite; Machu Picchu was filled with Incan temples and huge meticulously cut stones that formed this epic site.